Heart Balm~Just for You

Soothing, Simmering, Life-Shifting Poems and Activities

Charlotte "Sista C" Ferrell

The Peace and Love Poet

authorHOUSE®

AuthorHouse™
1663 Liberty Drive
Bloomington, IN 47403
www.authorhouse.com
Phone: 1 (800) 839-8640

Published by AuthorHouse 01/21/2017

ISBN: 978-1-5246-5843-4 (sc)

Contents

Acknowledgements

There are sounds etched deep in my heart. It's Mama's sweet bedtime medleys of gospel hymns and nursery rhymes. It's her and *Grandma Charlotte's voices reading stories, and* coaching me to learn memory verses for Sunday school. It's their joyful laughter when I won a 'huge' peppermint cane for reciting "I'm my Mama's little darling." I deeply appreciate the way Grandpa (James Brown - *not the famous singer*), maintained his parenting tradition of having me teach him something I learned at school every day. Before 'pre-K' existed in tiny Parsons, KS, they had "the lady across the street" give me tap dance and reading lessons. This led to my being a 'reading buddy' for younger children as a second grader and a lifetime passion for teaching others to read.

Many of my poems have a thread of social justice or social consciousness. Growing up in Kansas City, life was infused with discussions about civil rights, the strengths and pitfalls of political candidates, and our responsibility to stand up for what we believed in. Aside from church, my parents, Aljeane and Verne Burleson, were involved in the PTA, Yates branch YWCA, and the Neighborhood Action Group. Though their examples, we learned the importance of community involvement, service and making sure that others understand important issues. Each of these organizations supported my early explorations in writing and hosting events. Whenever I got a 'B' in any subject, Daddy always said, "That's good, but I want to see an 'A' next time." He was passionate about our getting the most from our education. As a Depression-era teen, he dropped out of school to work so his sister could go to cosmetology school. As I grew up, Aunt Wayne not only kept Mama's, my sister's and my hair styled, she introduced me to the forerunner of social media – the society news pages. She showed me how to address invitations, craft press releases and label photos in albums. Amazingly, she sent everybody she knew a card for every holiday, and included a dollar or more. Knowing how much joy those cards ignited definitely inspired me to start writing and giving tribute poems as gifts.

My brothers (Verne Jr., Stanley and Leslie Burleson), my sister, Lillian Bittaye, and my children (Ato, Alimayu and Charell Bonds) electrically charge my life with ideas, hope and motivation. Their love, trust, inquiries and respect are my heart balm and soul fuel. My children re-kindle memories of my grandparents' and parents' loving nature. Ato with his son, Daren; and Charell with her son, Omari, are raising creative, confident children who enthusiastically share their songs, poems, acting, or other skills at church, community, and school events. Chef Alimayu regularly spices up my spoken word events with finger licking good culinary creations and generous hospitality. Ato, a web designer, listens to my goals, patiently proofs my work, and designs beautiful, functional websites or promotional materials. Charell, an emerging health professional, transforms my stress to sunshine, fulfilling endless requests for help with logistics, videotaping or whatever is needed.

Hugs! Sincere, warm hugs generate precious "heart balm" from fellow poets who share the mic at Mustardseed, TPC, and other venues. My actress, "fairy Godmother", Virginia Capers and the L.A. "Godfather of poetry", Sunji Ali shifted my gears from being a shy, seat-hugging writer to a bold, performing, ensemble poet in 1991, at a time when I was still recuperating from a head injury and barely able to remember lines. Through them I learned to appreciate and laud what each person brings to the table, or 'mic' and how poetry helps us to impart history, culture, education, motivation and our faith. Allie Tolliver, a dearly beloved, departed friend, shared her velvet voice and forthright opinion to the writing, recording and workshop activities. Axe-man, Hilliard Wilson was the first musician to listen to and discuss my spoken words then create background music that gets people swaying, clapping or even dancing. The "Just for You- Jazzy Spoken Word" CD has some of his music and some created by Greg Cook and my producer- mentor, Mark Cargill. Over the period that I have been working on *Heart Balm~ Just for You,* the poets and musicians that have most frequently welcomed me to their venues include Shirley Simmons, Richard Jones (RIP), Matilda and April Haywood, De-Poet, Tu Nook, Carla Clark, Larry Robinson and the Crew Band. I deeply appreciate the support of Culver Palms U.M.C. (Culver City, CA), and St. Paul's U.M.C (Redondo Beach) and their Pastors (especially, Dr. Se Hee Han, and Rev. Lynette Fuka) who have welcomed me as a poet, storyteller, and peace art event coordinator.

Heartbalm~Just for You, has some quotes by Rev. Dr. Michael and Rickie Byars Beckwith, leaders of the Agape International Spiritual Center who consistently extol the values of love, creativity, forgiveness, patience, persistence, peace and sacred service. They have helped me find my voice and comfort level in expressing spiritual principles without being preachy or judgmental. Rickie B.B. inspired me to work more with children through regularly having me do poetry and writing activities with her Kuumba Kids. Likewise, Rev. Leon Campbell and Catherine Hammond of the Agape Family and Youth Ministry have given me opportunities to engage the elementary and pre-teen youth in several of the activities found in this book. Ms. Sylvia Harbin, a phenomenal public school teacher took poetry to a new level in language arts when she and I did weekly discussions with 1st graders about issues such as civil rights, non-violence, justice, and peace then had them write free verse poems. Between the start of the Season of Non-violence in January, and its end, April 4, the children collectively wrote over 100 poems and affirmed their certification as Ambassadors of Peace and Love. The Women's Ministry at Christ Our Redeemer A.M.E. (Pastors Mark and Hermia S. Whitlock) enabled my jazzy spoken word and journaling activities to soar at sea during a three- day cruise. At an inter-generational singles conference at COR, youth and seniors wrote blues and love poems after I shared some of mine and they surprised each other with the depth of their expressions. I have been challenged to make sure my poems 'make sense' by *the Information Diva*, Deborah Thorne who professes not to like poetry but has frequently incorporated my tribute poems and activities in her networking mixers, visioning workshops and other events.

Writing these acknowledgements has anchored my confidence that the activities that follow each chapter in **Heart Balm~ Just for You** are seriously tried and true. After a soul - searching retreat led by my social worker friend, Lisa Futrell-Williams, I received love-notes, thank you cards and invitations from people who felt they made breakthroughs in forgiveness or friendship during my guided visioning-and poetic journaling sessions. Recently, I read excerpts from the book, and asked participants in the Joy of Manifestation Family's morning conference call to comment on the activities. Putting my little baby out there was scary but the responses bathed it with love and comments such as, "Where and how soon can I get the book?" I thank Muriel Shabazz, founder of the morning "Oath Call", for her vote of confidence in welcoming me as a recurring Monday host.

Ms. Capers had our Lafayette West. Players Ensemble memorize and regularly perform "A Dream Deferred", by Langston Hughes. The desire to bring words to life and have them inspire or motivate people to be more loving, peaceful and creative led me (at 65) to 'go back to school' and pursue the deferred dream of becoming a filmmaker. I appreciate The Art Institute of CA-LA for great, hands-on digital cinema and broadcasting courses. And, I am especially grateful for the instructors Oscar

Gonzales, Steve Gerbson, John Rosenberg, Will Aldis, Jonathan LeMond, and Tina Mabry who encouraged my endeavors to create movies that transcend doom, gloom and violence to deftly deal with social issues, and reflect values such as love, joy, peace, hope, forgiveness and perseverance. Thank You.

Introduction

Heart balm - Just for You demonstrates what happens when you say yes to creativity and let it have its way. Instead of writing a CD insert for my *Just for You-Jazzy Spoken Word CD*, I was inspired to write a book. The book's twelve chapters are built around the poem's key thoughts, or stanzas. While the poem emerged quickly, the book has gestated long enough to birth a few babies.

One problem I identified during this creative pause was the presence of another 'baby' trying to make its way through. Prior to writing the poem, "Just for You", I was organizing material for a book and workshop series to be named, *Heart Balm*. As I discussed and shared the material at business, cultural and spiritual gatherings, the confusion dissolved. There is no conflict, these babies will be birth-mates. I decided to restructure the book as a poetry-centered self-development book, *Heart Balm~Just for You*: soothing, simmering, life-shifting poems. Why? Because each of these poems have emanated from my heart. Reflecting upon them has led to shifts in consciousness, or healing, refreshing experiences. Writing through, working through and experiencing the activities with individuals and in group settings has established confidence that they are "do-able" and beneficial. They do not carry claims, such as 'relieves pain in 15 minutes', but they follow the ancient health intention set by Hippocrates, "To do no harm."

The *Just for You –Jazzy Spoken Word* CD presents nine of the poems that 'jump started' this book. At events, people have danced, discussed or extensively reflected on how the words are "just for them." It is available at www.cdbaby.com/artist/charlottesistacferrell!.

This book is organized with each stanza of the poem, "Just for You", organized as a chapter that includes poems related to that sentiment. Each chapter ends with a set of activities that people have affirmed as making them feel many of the following ways: *inspired, empowered, energized, creative, loved, loving, confident, or capable.*

HEART BALM IS...?

Heart balm is a sentiment of the heart.
Applying heart balm doesn't mean something is wrong.
Heart balm is openness
Openness to the idea that your heart is a source of *balm*
Heart balm is openness to helping others survive their wars.
Heart balm is an ocean of love
It flows out to kiss the horizon, then returns to hydrate the shore
It brings eerie calm or an exhilarating roar.

Out of the heart pours the issues of life.
Within the heart lies the balm to calm and avoid strife.
Through heart balm, boiling lava is transformed into hot tubs.
Hot tubs are steamy - warmer than a lake - but livable, capable;
Soaking in them opens pores and creates new capillaries.
Heart balm is eating honey – like *Winnie the Poo-* without packing on pounds.
You can feast on it and still fit through all your doors.

Heart balm glides the way and cushions tight places.
Heart balm prevents ragged entry ways from ripping your clothes,
        or compressing your soul.
Heart balm is applicable via the ear or eye.
Heart balm is directly absorbable on the fly.
The side effects of heart balm are good and all good.

Heart balm is the stuff that you find helpful in this book.
It goes well by candle light or while sipping a cup of tea.
It goes well with cabbage or fruits of the sea.

Heart balm is safe for children and youth.

Apply liberally when you encounter situations uncouth.

Its essence is invisible but carries a special scent,

It has ways of warming and relieving one when bent.

But note: its substance finds anchor within as sweet fruit.

Heart balm is a treasured gift for sharing and exchanging views;

Ultimately it can be enjoyed around the earth with all its hues.

*Balm, an ointment or curative substance that heals bruises and scars; any of several aromatic plants.

JUST FOR YOU – the poem that launched a book

Have you ever had anyone do anything just for you?
I mean,
Just for you?
Have you ever had anyone write anything just for you?
I mean,
Just for you?
Well!

This poem is .... just for you.
It is for you with cheer for your feelings to be held dear.
It is for you with hope for your dreams to prosper and float.

This poem is... just for you.
It is for your encouragement as you pound the pavement.
It is for your courage as you release fear and turn a new page.

This poem is ... just for you.
It is for you with hugs and smiles right here
            or across the miles.
It is for you with wishes and more
            as you open that new door.

This poem is ... just for you.
It is for your peace as you take in all life has to teach.
It is for your wealth as you bask in excellent health.

This poem is...just for you.
It is for you with love that is blessed from above.
It is for you with bliss that never ever goes amiss.
This poem is...just for you.

Chapter 1
Have you ever had anyone do anything just for you?

Just in time; just at the right time, there are people who make things happen for us all the time with no expectation of anything in return. This chapter is dedicated to the folk who pour the priceless gifts of "themselves" into the lives of family members, friends, students, members, clients and co-workers. In contrast to the next chapter which shares tribute poems written for specific people or special occasions, these poems are written about the characteristics of doing something no matter what or for no special reason.

After reading these selections, perhaps you will feel inspired to think of someone who has enriched your life or lightened your load. That person may no longer be around or available to you but thinking about them may lead you do something that makes someone's day *just 'because.'* As best- selling author of *Who's Got Your Back,* Keith Ferrazzi states, "The idea isn't to find yourself another environment for tomorrow, but to be constantly creating the environment and community you want for yourself, no matter what may occur." Casting off doubt or worry and doing something for someone else regularly is a simple way to run with this idea.

DOING IT ANYWAY

Doing it anyway
Doing without weariness
Doing it despite and no matter what
Is the highest order of the day
Doing it with joy
Doing it when jackhammers and jacks of all trades
Show up at the door amidst your quiet time

Doing it anyway
Doing it without compliments or wishing for them
Doing it unfettered by ungrateful reception
Doing it without knowing how it will be received
Doing it with excellence, your inner self to please

Doing it anyway
Doing it with diligence and pride
Doing it with life force and love intertwined
Doing it and moving on
Doing it and seeding hope in rain
Doing it with arms welcoming the sunshine
Doing it anyway

Rebirthing I Worthiness

You are the beloved of your innermost heart
With each beat a thunderous reminder sounds
Yet sometimes it falls into the abyss
The abyss of misconceptions about "I" worthiness
The abyss of mistrust fed by ill conceptions
Of how marvelous it would be if you felt fantastic about "I"

You are the "I" that has smelled the sacred essence of fertile dreams
You are the "I" that has felt brilliance brimming over with solutions
Solutions to family matters, financial matters, environmental matters
Solutions to the issues of the day that matter most for human survival
You are the "I" that has voluntarily surrendered its voice,
Surrendered its power,
Surrendered its sweetness

Now step into the bliss of birthing "I" from its cocoon
Now step into the bliss of birthing the fruit of your Yes
Now step into the bliss of acknowledging "I" love with content
Acknowledging love and appreciation for your gifts as "I"
Acknowledging love and appreciation for the "I" in your integrity
Acknowledging love and appreciation for the "I" that has:
Abundant creativity, abundant health, abundant joy,
Abundant generosity, abundant prosperity, and abundant peace
And so it is for "I" and "I".

CAN DO

I do
You do
He, she or it does
We do

We do take up the reins again
Dodge all the raindrops and cold wind
We saddle up and move out
Reflect and know we have clout
We travel at warp speed
Unfettered by rumors of lack or need
Yesterday's news is today's resolution
Arm in arm, we mirror earth's revolutions

Round and round beam the woe tales
Up and upward wind our victory trails
Soft and steady a new cadence drum-urges
I can
You can
He, she and it can
We can

WE ARE

We are able to do exceedingly well
Drumming, beating, tapping the snare
New fields of dreams appear and take root
New rainbows arc and arch bridges of hope
At the end of the rainbow the gold may be gone
At the end of your wits the deal may be fresh

Fresh ideas, fresh deeds
Fresh ideas, fresh appeals
Just under the rocky mound
       Remove the rocks from your assigned plot
       Clear the area within your roped-off ridge

Dig and clear; grade and sift
Till until the rich brown earth appears
Till and toll with a rhythmic work song
Harvest and export with a philanthropic heart
Pull up your pail
Fill up your basket
Abundance is overflowing wells and hills

READY FOR ACTION

Blessed and ready
I am blessed and ready for action this day
No nagging phone calls or commercial cares will cast me astray
I am blessed and ready for this day
God has invited me to come out and play
Play on the playing field of giants and geniuses
Pinch hit and run, bring all the runners home

I am blessed and ready for action this day
Callers are on line with offers and solutions
Judgment and discretion entwine the balance beam
Good, and more good, flow my way

I speak into existence fruit and flowers
Wonderful essence and substance to pave the way
The path under my feel winds toward wisdom and riches
My underpinnings rise to the surface as stud walls and support beams
My heart is assured and resolved to achieve its purpose
I am anchored and well girded for gale winds and high tide
I am blessed and ready for action this day

CHARLOTTE "SISTA C" FERRELL

GIVING THANKS FOR YOU

You are a gem in life's jewelry case
Sometimes you may feel *lackluster* or
Feel as if the show lights are in the wrong place
Yet in truth you are a marvelous example of grace
So, today I'm saying, "Thanks for you."

Thank you for all you do, whether
Encouraging, teaching, leading, preaching or parenting
Your life gives someone a special view.
Today you took time to rise and shine again
You shared a smile and got hope blooming

Working harder or smarter to catch up the slack
You block frustration and reverse fear of lack
Thank **you** for just being **you**
Thank you again for all that you do.

RE-PATTERNING PRETTINESS

Sunny days
Clear, clean beaches
Bodies from Self to Vogue
Blemish-free
Beacon to and bait us

Pretty patterns with Madison Avenue swatches
       Swatch watches
       Paraffin-dipped hands, pedicured toes
       Tripping egos, breaking hearts
       And handbags
Until we hit the re-boot button

Tripping us back to natural wonder
Wonderful appreciation of smiling eyes
Warm hands
Warm hearts
Whatever the wrapping

Ushering in awakened appreciation
Prying open pretty petals of
       Sacred customs
       Secrets shared and kept
       Offers to sail past the mundane
Making love, making jazz,
Making homemade fudge,
Making smiles, making pretty
Re-patterning Prettiness

Stepping Through Kwanzaa

We're stepping through the week, celebrating Kwanzaa
Activating the Nguzo Saba.
Standing in a unified circle, we will launch Umoja
We will wind our way along the Kujichagulia path of self-determination
Collect ourselves through Ujima as we commit to help solve each other's problems
And build strong, enduring communities.

Then we will arrive, regally at the mid-point,
Standing on the balancing beam of Ujamaa,
Ready to break ground for a new economic harvest
        of sister-dreams, brother-dreams, ancestor-connecting visons,
Finally coming to fruition and profiting us for our labor.
Becoming like Joseph, the relative that uses new-found riches to
Rescue our distant or estranged family members From the ravages of poverty, parent-
less-ness, war, disease and despair.

We will generate a new Nia as we pursue our purpose, Find new ways to build and
develop together.
As emanations of our Creator, we press in
Gleaning the blessings of Kuumba:
Breathing in, bearing down,
Birthing beautiful, beneficial strategies, stories, stores, and sounds

As we remember and re-affirm our faith in God, we joyfully:
Stand on Imani and fully open our hearts to really believe in ourselves
Stand on Imani and believe there is no-thing too hard for us.
Our Christ consciousness has given us the power,
Given us the authority to do all things, even reclaim our greatness.

Dedicated with continual appreciation to Dr. Maulana Karinga who had the insight, care and concern to create Kwanzaa (and the Nguzo Saba) as a holiday for African Americans to reflect upon and continually develop our culture and communities. Originally written as a tribute to Deborah Thorne, the Information Diva, for her Kids First and She-e-o services.

Chapter 1: Activities
Doing Something for Someone

Doing something for someone involves getting off the balance beam of wondering, "Should I or shouldn't I?" When we have an unction (inner urge) to do something special for someone, the first thing we often have to override is that humanly *worry* that "maybe they will take it the wrong way." Or, the self-centered question, "Why doesn't someone do this for me?" One treasured thought from, *The Answer is You* by philosopher-spiritual leader, Rev. Michael Bernard Beckweth, is that we only get to keep what we give away. An old gospel hymn has a similar message,

> *The more you give, the more he gives to you.*
> *Just keep on giving because it's really true...*
> *You can't beat God giving, no matter what you do.*

Open a computer box, a new telephone or printer and the first thing you see is the 'Quick Start Guide.' Consider the following activities as a quick start for doing something special for someone.

1. How can you apply this often-repeated quote from ***Alice in Wonderland***:

    "Alice laughed: "There's no use trying," she said; "one can't believe impossible things." "I daresay you haven't had much practice," said the Queen. "When I was younger, I always did it for half an hour a day. Why, sometimes I've believed as many as six impossible things before breakfast."

2. Vision or Reflect: Identify one person or cause that you are able to do something for. The someone who could benefit may be in the next seat, room or building. Think of the time(s) you may have thought "what they need is __"; or someone needs to do something about ___." Picture or imagine

your *someone*'s joy in having a new pen, clean shirt or your special dish. Or, if you have *teckie* skills, how someone you know would benefit from a simple, patient tutorial on how to use their cell phone or a software update. Picture a specific person and something you can do for them sincerely, unconditionally - perhaps even anonymously.

3. Take action. Stop pondering about doing something for someone and J.D.I. (just do it).

4. Keep the flow going by regularly identifying supposedly *impossible things* then drawing on resources that can help you build a team to accomplish them. Set an intention and start on one today.

Chapter 2
Have you ever had anyone write anything just for you?

Have you ever had anyone write anything just for you? Since 1992 I have written and presented over a hundred tribute poems commemorating birthdays, anniversaries, graduations, business launches and cultural celebrations for family members, friends, teachers, leaders and other creative artists. Whether surprised or expecting the poem, people always express joy, gratitude and appreciation. In this chapter I am sharing a selection of poems that illustrate that there is no set format for a poem - just the intention to share an honest, positive expression.

    I absolutely love the experience of writing tribute poems. It is a humbling, exciting, nurturing adventure in being open to the words Spirit reveals to capture qualities or aspects of a person's life. Writing something about someone provides an opportunity to activate the faith principle of "speaking those things that are not as if they were." You can call forth something that someone may not even have seen in yourself. Every time I perform *Sista Friends* someone asks for a copy or tells me how much it makes them think about their sister, or the way they would like to be as a sister.

My tribute poems have their roots in an African poetry genre called *Praise Song,* which the Encyclopedia Britannica summarizes as follows:

> *Praise song, one of the most widely used <u>poetic forms in Africa</u>; a series of laudatory epithets applied to gods, men, animals, plants, and towns that capture the essence of the object being praised. Professional bards, who may be both praise singers to a chief, and court historians of their tribe, chant praise songs...*

"praise song". Encyclopædia Britannica. Encyclopædia Britannica Online. Encyclopædia Britannica Inc., 2016. Web. 07 Nov. 2016 <https://www.britannica.com/art/praise-song>.

SISTA FRIENDS

Sista friends, Sista friends
Friends who are there at the end of the day
Those a call away, when disaster strikes,
When the big question gets popped,
The promotion finally comes through,
Or, when you are just feeling blue

Sista Friends know what time it is
You don't need to constantly explain yourself
Even when you're fronting
They smile and edge you on
But pull your coat when your slip is showing
Let you know if your hair is out of place
Before you fall out upon the world's stage

Sista Friends call your kids theirs
They are not afraid to speak up
Whether you are overboard with spoiling
Or sharing the rod a little too much
They step in as aunties, extra moms,
Grannies with a gentle touch.
Not crowding your authority,
But letting you know
They've got good intentions on their mind.
An extra meal, one more pair of shoes
Are no big matter, they'd do it anytime!

Sista Friends, Sista Friends
Have got your back through thick and thin
When you move, they bring boxes
When you're being moved, they move to step in
No streets for you, no shelters for you
They couldn't sleep!
While they have a home –
You know, so do you

Sista Friends, Sista Friends
Call you up to share good news
If soup is on sale
Or a good workshop is being held
They want you to get in on it too

Sista Friends, Sista Friends
Sometimes have to bury hatchets too
Errors are made, the wrong thing is said
But under God's heaven a path has been made
Just be the one to say," I'm sorry", and
Know in your heart your sister is sorry too
Let by-gones be gone to keep your friendship true.

Celebrating the Captivating, Enervating Ms. C

Like a golden winged angel
You have sprinkled golden thoughts
Into our heads and upon our paths
Burned a desire for drama into our breasts
Run lines with us until we could stand industry tests

With strong arms you have borne us
To mind-boggling heights
Then flown near until we lost our fear
And took charge of our own courses
Stopped by from time to time
To rock our babies in the night

With a firm stand
You've kept hold of God's hand
Always affirming hope
No matter what the medic's prognosis
Speaking dreams into reality
Planting in us what your father taught you
That "can't" is an animal too lazy to try

Happy Birthday to You
May God continually bless you
With Angel champions surrounding you
And stars twinkling around you

A birthday poem written and presented Sept. 26, 2001, for my dear surrogate mother, auntie, friend and mentor, Mrs. Virginia Capers - a Diva forever sharing her home, heart and talent.

CHARLOTTE "SISTA C" FERRELL

REVEREND YES

You raise your arms and Ys project
You carry and convey our "**Yes**" directly to God's door
Yes, you said, "**Yes**".
Surrendered to the vision
Through you, many have escaped from prison

Yes, Rev. Michael, you are God's light
A messenger, freeing all from the tyranny of *scripted right.*
You reveal righteousness from a spiritual plane
Share thoughts on Liberation that are wholesome and sane

Yes, your books, likeness and sounds abound
Gently you walk among us proclaiming *Holy Ground*
Your "**Yes**" is a whisper,
Your "**Yes**" is a roar
Either way there is no doubt it will help us to soar
Into our "Yes", you speak the Word for wholeness
Into our "**Yes**", you declare that all is well
Whether taking that breath, or releasing life's bonds
You welcome and offer prayer with a motion of your arms
Angel, Messenger, Servant and Helmsman
Your leadership is a testament to focused intent
Voicing your visions,
You consistently inspire us to create or invent

A tribute poem written for Rev. Dr. Michael Bernard Beckwith, Spiritual Director of the Agape International Spiritual Center. His love-centered, non-judgmental teaching and mentoring on spiritual principles and practices transforms lives.

Hail Queen Sister, Musical Director

Hail Queen, Soul Sister Number One
Hail Mother, Friend, Marvelous Musical Director
Hail to the regal-voiced global lady, Rickie B.B.
Dr. Rickie Byars Beckwith, precious daughter of God

Your left foot deftly pats two-four time;
You make a slight nod and sax unwinds
Your right hand beacons five-part harmony to ascend
Then feet start flying and skirts swirling,
You seed sweetness with a harmonious blend
You beam as your children, fosterlings, cherubs or stalwarts
Take to the stage, rocking the house from end to end

Your perfection is evident but none seem hard pressed
Joyfully artists venture from global mileposts to Agape steps
Unconditional Love powerfully drives your soul train
You move from Nepal through New York to Kuumba, among the best
Earnestly hugging folk making them all feel loved and blessed

Queenly, you shift from quiet to calmly stern
Situation by situation you discern which way to turn
Anointed composer, angelic vocalist, nurturing wife
What a Revelation is expressed throughout your life

I wrote and presented this tribute poem to "Rickie BB" at her KUUMBA birthday celebration, Oct. 10, 2010. She directs music and projects with humility, balancing intense focus with an assuring smile.

CHARLOTTE "SISTA C" FERRELL

You're Pretty Wonderful –
Happy Mother's Day

You're the one who carried the weight
        up to that special birth date
You keep us under your protective wings
        when life's problems produce stings
You're pretty wonderful – yes You are

You wash faces and hands; pots and pans,
        whether you're tired or not,
        even when you're not feeling so hot...
You're pretty wonderful – yes You are

You figure out math and science homework,
        and even how to tie Scout knots
You make a pledge – You carry it out
Time and time you come through without a doubt
You're pretty wonderful – yes You are

You're one who goes to the beach,
        carries a peach, and find time to teach
The one who teaches how to cross the street
        and deal with the unique folks in life you meet
You're pretty wonderful, yes You are

You're one who prays and reflects every day,
          keeps your resolve whenever others may say:
"Your child is this," or, "Your child is *that*."
When it's all said and done, You've *got our back*
You're pretty wonderful – yes You are
You are truly one blessed by God – Yes you are!

Thank God For Fathers

Thank God for fathers
Thank you for the fathers who have followed your Word in fathering children
Those who have invited you into their relationships
Who have modeled your covenant in their family covenant

Thank you God
For fathers who have braved first the whip,
Then the whip-like conditions of various workplaces
To put fruit in refrigerators; beans in pots
Meat and bread on tables
Thank you for those who aren't too proud to
Serve delicacies to their families and friends

Thank you God
For our men who have been so misunderstood
Who media have scraped, sniped and discouraged
For their courage to own their own images
To re-claim their heritage
To master sports and sport top academic honors
To build careers and own businesses
To stand on point and bring up the rear
To wash little hands and mend broken hearts

Thank you God
For those men who lavish fatherly care on children not their own
Who have the courage and patience to deal with sour attitudes,
hot tempers and terrible tongues
Thank you God for those who step up to the plate

As coaches, mentors, teachers and friends
Having the discipline to dry little girl's and women's tears without twisting their lives

Thank you God
For the fathers who seek your face and fall before it
Who invite you to walk with them.
Who invite you to talk with them.
Who invite you to sing with them.
Who invite you to work and mend with the
Who invite you to teach with them. Who invite you preach with them
Who invite you to be their Father and Friend

Thank you God for Fathers!
And thank you especially for the fathers, grandfathers, uncles, brothers, cousins, pastors and friends YOU sent to share fatherly love with me.

Dedicated at Mustardseed Ministries International's Juneteenth Celebration 2002 in Los Angeles, and aired on KJLH as a promotion for a Father's Day event at Derrick's Restaurant. Charles Wade III was so determined to have a copy for his father that came to the station and ordered a CD a month before it was recorded.

FRIENDSHIP TOOK ON A NEW NAME

Friendship took on a new name today
You came into the room
You began moving with purpose, moving with grace
Nothing is quite the same in our place

Friendship grew to new heights the day
You stood on the line
Came out of your comfort zone
Helped remove the stones along the way

Friendship adds lace to life's seams every day
That your love pours water for the thirsty,
Sews, pastes, cuts, binds and delivers limited resources
Encourages the hesitant and troubled to pray

Friendship, your friendship has made us complete
Like cobbler and fruitcake, it's *heartwarming* sweet
Given freely, it has helped – gosh – a plenty
To draw others near to serve and cheer many

Friendship, your friendship has helped us stand on the line
To endure the high and low tides of Mother Time

MARY MCLEOD BETHUNE
– a Woman Attuned

This is a call and response poem enjoyed at many events.

Mary (poet)
McLeod Bethune (group)
Mary (poet)
McLeod Bethune (group)

Mary McLeod Bethune
Was a woman totally to her time attuned?
Was a woman totally to our people's needs attuned

Education was her marching hymn
She moved across the country from end to end
Gathering support for her school after a lifetime of teaching
To many it sounded like she was preaching

Mary (poet)
McLeod Bethune (group)
Mary (poet)
McLeod Bethune (group)

Blessed to have a formal education
She decided to stay within this nation'
Served lunch to the homeless, counseled the poor
Got a Sunday school going even sang behind the prison door

Mary (poet)
McLeod Bethune (group)
Mary (poet)
McLeod Bethune (group)

July 10, 1875 gave rise to a South Carolina star
Before 1955 she helped break the color bar
Had lunch with presidents
Kept her name among the current events
Held to God's unfailing hand with faith
Building schools and hospitals under grace

Mary (poet)
McLeod Bethune (group)
Mary (poet)
McLeod Bethune (group)

Mary McLeod Bethune
Forged a link with Cookman College
Made Bethune-Cookman an Institute for lifelong knowledge
Made women's organizations look beyond class and privilege
Gained a seat on Truman's Committee of Twelve
Had the National Council of Negro Women into politics delve
Under Coolidge, Hoover and Roosevelt
Child welfare, education, employment and housing
Were issues over which she worked up a sweat
Mary McLeod Bethune – may we only with you stay attuned

Mary (poet)
McLeod Bethune (group)
Mary (poet)
McLeod Bethune (group)

    *Originally I wrote and performed this poem for SoulVisions **Front Line Poets'** Women's Month Celebration in 2005 at Shabazz Restaurant, LA. Since then, I have presented it for the National Council of Negro Women, and for several Black History Month and Juneteenth celebrations. People of all ages and races enjoy the call and response activity, and often request to "do it one more time."*

JAZZY POMP

Girrrll, did you hear that?
That's a mean keyboard funk line in *Pomp and Circumstance*
Yeah, Joe put a sweet downbeat in the upright processional
Pomp and Circumstance celebrated with culture

You know our celebration would not be complete
Without a little touch of cultural class
It was there, subtle - not overt
Fingers kissing treasured chords
Dancing across the traditional keyboard

Thank you for the joy you jammed into this special day
You wove wonder with wisdom
In your own inimitable way
Gave the waves of caps and gowns
Electrifying energy
In the heat of the day

Written during a graduation ceremony at Charles R. Drew University of Medicine and Science, L.A., as the incredibly humble, ingenious, Director of Music, Professor Joseph Williams wove African American cultural threads into the traditional" Pomp and Circumstance" march. I presented Joe with a copy in his classroom weeks later.

PAYING TRIBUTE TO YOUR SPIRIT, MAMA

I'm paying tribute to your Spirit, Mama
Paying tribute to your spirit of love, laughter
argument, and encouragement

I'm paying to your Spirit, Mama
Now that you've gone
I told you that I love you, but it's not enough
The words are too few for the essence of You
I'm paying tribute to your Spirit, Mama

I'm paying tribute to your Spirit, Mama
Your tireless hands that fashioned new dresses
when I longed for the ones at Macy's
that cost more than Daddy made

I'm paying tribute to your Spirit, Mama
Your endless treks to sales, downtown, over town
T o the Plaza, to wherever you could get:
Five pairs of shoes, five sets of clothes,
ten days of groceries on a postman's biweekly pay

I'm paying tribute to your Spirit, Mama
For facing freezing snowstorms, spending lonely nights at home
while your plight, to others, was generally unknown

I'm paying tribute to your Spirit, Mama
For ever reminding us to *slow down and smell the roses,*
Do one thing at a time
Wait upon the Lord and
Hear the quiet solutions He whispers at sunrise

I'm paying tribute to your Spirit, Mama
For the radiant way you faced the ravishes
of a painful, prolonged death
Defied depression and refused to cry
when the last strands of hair left
Set your vision on where you were going
rather than where you had been

I'm paying tribute to your Spirit, Mama
For the indirect beauty you let flow from within,
The loving way you dismissed me
to go back to my family
and accept The End

I'm paying tribute to your Spirit, Mama
For crossing the gulf between your Heavenly rest
and this earthly test
To give me answers to the questions
To stand at the finish line and cheer me on
To coach the matches, the enemy would have won

I'm just paying tribute to *your Spirit,* Mama.

Dedicated to the memory and appreciation of my Mama - Aljeane Brown Burleson: Mama, Nana, Ms. Aljeane, Auntie, sister, cousin, counselor, friend and extra mom to many. As it grew close to Mother's Day, a year after Mama made her transition; I was driving in LA and was so overtaken by tears I had to pull off the road. As soon as I got home, I sat down and this soothing poem came from that wonderful place called, 'somewhere.' Later, it became my first video poem.

LADY LISA

As Lisa comes to mind many words fill your soul
Lady, Friend, Encourager, Prayer Warrior, Bold
Bold woman of faith, love and hope
Fun lady to travel the road and ride the airwaves
For *getting to the root* of things, she is always brave

Lady Lisa has a distinctive laugh
It is contagious, it is unique
It can make you fall right off your feet
She tells jokes, she makes life happy
She is the one to call if you are feeling crappy

Lady Lisa is a creative explorer
Forget texting and driving she captures sunrises
While driving the road she captures beautiful surprises
Exploring the limits of Photo shop and canvas
She brings new life to events small and vast

Lady Lisa is a builder and restorer
She brings bandages and balm to heal scrapes or sores
For others lives she has helped weave safety nets
Now she is blessed to probe and seal her launching nest
Sooja is off on a blessed adventure

Written especially for my friend Lisa Futrell-Williams for the 'bon voyage party' in support of her journey to Korea to explore her heritage. 8/12/11

Chapter 2: Activities
Have you ever had anyone write anything just for you?

Writing something about or for someone always seems to flow best after a period of quiet reflection. It is helpful to brainstorm a few characteristics you would like to highlight without giving any particular preference to any specific one. It is sometimes helpful - but not necessary - to have some details, colorful memorabilia, or photographs on hand. When someone asks me to create a tribute poem for a person or event I do at least six of the eight things listed below:

1. **Reflect**: picture the person as you know them, or from a description. Make a few notes or a doodle that help you visualize them.
2. **List:** Make some simple lists:
    a. personality traits;
    b. characteristics or attributes about the person or event
    c. favorite or notable things or activities
3. **Identify** the purpose for the poem, i.e. is it a birthday gift, memorial or award?
4. **Write some phrases** that incorporate 1 and 2 above – initially, just enjoying the fun of expressing yourself and see what natural rhythm or rhyme patterns emerge. There is no necessity to rhyme.
5. **Review** what you have written; re-consider how the phrases may need to be grouped or re-expressed to match the goals identified for the poem, or its tempo.
6. **Read** your tribute poem aloud, maybe in a mirror; maybe to a family member or friend. Request and open yourself to receiving constructive criticism.
7. **Follow your heart** regarding how you think your authentic words will make the person feel.
8. Type or record the poem and give it to them.

Chapter 3
For you with cheer for your feelings to be held dear

Feelings - everyone has them but often we spend a lot of time denying or feeling anxious about them. Sometimes we let fear override our desire to say or write something that would give us a great deal of pleasure to express. We needlessly worry whether expressing our feelings will lead to being rejected, hurt, or misunderstood. Brother Ishmael Tetteh, Director of the Ethereal Mission in Ghana, and international speaker, asserts that there is joy in personally enjoying our feelings. If the words we express make us feel love and joy, that is enough. Don't expect or require anything in return, he advises.

When I first wrote "for you with cheer for your feelings to be held dear," I had an image of happiness or contentment over having someone cherish my feelings. I did not have any particular person in mind - just the feeling of contentment about the sacredness and specialness of unveiling feelings where they were appreciated. During the 'double gestation" period of living with the thoughts I am sharing here, I came to realize there is no necessity for the receiver to "hold" my words in the same spirit or with the same feeling quality as I give them. The cheer or joy is in releasing what

I would like to express honestly, and with no intention of malice or injury. This means expressions of feelings do not have to be about love, romance, 'hooking up' or regaining something. The important thing is authentically sharing what is on your heart, not to be confused with giving a person a piece of your mind. Expressing your feelings about your beliefs, emotions and concerns are important ways of avoiding stagnation. Learning to explore and regularly express the full range of your feelings, *even if on paper that no one else ever sees*, is an extremely valuable, joy-filled personal experience.

Sharing expressions of our feelings only becomes a problematic, painful or troubling experience when we coerce or expect someone to reciprocate or feel exactly the same way. When people's feelings are affirmed by pledges or vows it is probably a good idea to treat them as 'emerging", living documents. Sometimes we block or reject positive feelings that friends, relatives or *others* have for us because we are pre-occupied with trying to 'make' someone else feel the same thing for us that we feel for them. Sometimes we keep our feelings in harm's way because we refuse to shift or transfer them from a source that is hostile or disrespectful. In North American culture (perhaps others, but this is 'my culture') a disproportionate amount of emphasis is place on romantic feelings. Worse, conversation in many social media sites center around how someone showed they "care" by giving them a valuable gift. Your feelings are your valuable gift. Enjoy holding and savoring those feelings and exploring their true nature. Sometimes people think they are in love with a teacher or doctor because they were the first people to help them accomplish something wonderful. The feelings are actually joy and gratitude, but in a culture that rarely explores these feelings, it is easy to confuse them as "love."

Your feelings are sometimes, *just for you.* Even when you consider them to be for or about others, they are still, just about you. The poems in this chapter reflect different ways of exploring these thoughts. I invite you to take a few moments after reading them to poetically explore and express *your feelings.*

LOVE NOTES ON LIFE

When the little nay say-er, gatekeepers of life's bad news
Seem to be emptying their innards on you
When the storm clouds of life
Seem to have parked over your head

Look up; look over...You've got gate-opening power
Your battle force is surrounding you
You just need to reach in
Reach in.
Instead of 'Intel' you've got God within
Reach in and receive the baton from grace
Timeless power is ready to glow from your face

Look around: Check the frowns,
Hair trigger tempers and curse-ridden replies
Have coroners counting unclaimed bodies
Crammed cemeteries with headstones, marked and unmarked
In a flash any one could go down

Look up, look around
There is a fountain of love ready to lift you
To a level where you have not been
Don't descent, ascend
Life's tests may bend, but renewed strength is within
You will win way before life's end

DOUBLE YES

They keep asking 'are we sure'?
Did we take enough time to make up our minds?
Did we get enough education?
Or, have enough fun?
The answer is "Yes, double Yes."

They ask if we have the sustainability
To last until perpetuity
Will we scramble and fuss,
Or can we hold on to "us"
When the tests of time begin to unfold
The answer is "Yes, double Yes."

What of the ties we have to careers and our crowd...
Shopping dates, movie nights, bowling leagues, card parties,
And better yet, customary family occasions
Can we re-schedule, budget and adjust our priorities?
The answer is "Yes, double Yes."

Do we take each other, with our fragile feelings
To have and to hold – to treasure like gold,
Until we slip into to life's higher ceiling?
The answer is "Yes, double Yes."

This poem is recorded with original music by Hilliard Wilson. Initially, I wrote it to commemorate Stanley and Beatrice's (my brother and sister-in-law) marriage on Mama's birthday. It continues to be a popular performance poem for weddings and anniversaries.

CHARLOTTE "SISTA C" FERRELL

MYSTERIOUS EYES

Sparkle, sparkle, wonderful eyes
She saw them sparkle when you smiled
What a breath of fresh air you bring
Your charm and style make her want to sing

Captain, friend, father, brother, mate
There is much curiosity prior to a date
Are you bound to some dear other?
Or, a free heart, in search of another?

Life and joy spring from your smile
Your strong limbs do not beguile
To hard work, you are no stranger
You've studied and sacrificed
Toiled to keep others out of danger

With a deft touch and subtle moves
You suggest how you'd make life smooth
Face, eyes and cheeks fashioned from above
To rise to the top,
You forged ahead with love
Never overtook others with a shove

Special star, shining ever brightly
Yes, she'd like to have you hold her tightly
Into the ether you may breathe,
"Let us not compromise solemn oaths by deeds,
Only if it's blessed, let us explore life's needs."

WHAT'S UP WITH HIM? –

What's up with him?
You know he could be the one
What's up with him?
You know your search could be done
What's up with him?
Love is never lost forever
What's up with him?
Your loneliness could be over

What's up with him?
You could be dancing in aisle ways
What's up with him?
Hope may be searching for you today
What's up with him?
You know he could be the one

What's up with him?
What's up with him?
What's up with him?

What's up with him?
You could be missing and not knowing
What's up with him?
Meals could grow to two hearts soaring

What's up with him?
He does not look like a clone
What's up with him?
He may love home, not to roam
What's up with him - what's up with him?

What's up with him?
No more fighting and crying
What's up with him?
You may be dancing and dining
What's up with him?
A new life could be building
What's up with him - what's up with him?
What's up with him?

This jazz 'performance poem' was inspired by John Coltrane's "A Love Supreme"

NO WASH AND WEAR FEELINGS

They've got wash and wear everything:
        underwear, shirts, skirts, hair!
Practically everything today is wash and wear
Except feelings

Please don't expect me to wash and wear my feelings
Like they're some old pair of sneakers
Like you can just pick them off the rack at Macy's
Or grab them up at midnight at a grocery store

My feelings are not a Madison Avenue commodity
They do not rise and fall like the stock market
        at the bid and nod of overzealous traders
My feelings are like private label wine,
        mellowing and awaiting a true connoisseur.

Feelings are to be expressed, not compressed.
Exploring and enjoying feelings is a gift
Expressing, showering or sharing them is free, not forced.
Feelings deserve to be more than dipped, flipped, tripped,
        or wrung and hung out to dry.
It is my cherished intention never to wash and wear your feelings
I will eternally appreciate your not washing and wearing mine.

CHARLOTTE "SISTA C" FERRELL

SMOOTHING THE EDGES

Red to orange to blue to white hot
Pain shooting, chomping, poking, making fun
Trying to assert and insert itself above hope and joy
Tearing and tossing nerves, frying them to medium rare

Pain is neither a figment of the imagination
Nor is it easily shifted or sifted away
"Give me your peace, your strength, your indie spirit,"
It demands, but your reserve shuts the door
Neither its banging, clanging or sleep robbery is sufficient

You are holding your peace
Writing, soaring, singing in the nearly spent healthy percent
You go within and find a reservoir
A reservoir that spills golden gel on the grinding joints
Showers the seething neurons with nature's own hydrants

You sing lullabies among the dendrites, calming them
Cooing and extracting the balm from dopamine receptors
Cancelling orders for medically approved silencers
That knit nice rows of nothingness while *purling* knots in kidneys
You find the rivulets of perfection and calming waterfalls emerge

THE THING ABOUT THE BLUES

The thing about the blues
  is that they always pick the worse time to come around.
They visit you at night, in nerves and pain,
  when all your friends have settled down.
Blues lay all their burdens on your dinner table,
  make you eat, then want for more.

The thing about the blues
is that they always pick the worse time to come around.
Blues will climb into your bed, make it so sad,
  you'll and get out and sleep down on the floor.
Blues can take a spelling test, get you so mixed up,
  you think s-m-i-l-e spells STRESS.

The thing about the blues
is that they always pick the worse time to come around
You can be dressing yourself for church, then find
hot tears running down your cheeks to spoil your clothes.
Blues can ruin a sunny day,
  make you think Miami May is Chicago in the snow.

The thing about the blues
Is that they will fight you till you send them someplace else.
  Send them on someplace else, now.
  The thing about the blues!

    CHARLOTTE "SISTA C" FERRELL

I recorded this poem with some fantastic musicians at Mark Cargill's studio. It is the first poem I braved performing at venues with my friends, Allie Tolliver -a velvet-voiced Blues diva, and L.A.'s Godfather of jazz-blues poetry, Sunji Ali.

WHEN I BID GOODBYE

When I bid my earthly body good-bye
And take my pathway to the sky
Dance one last dance
Serve some homemade pie
And dry the last tear from your eye

When I make my sojourn to the sky
No need to fuss, scurry, or lie
Review all the records
Then just try
To dry the last tear from your eye

When I do what some call die
And my words cease to fly
Bring on the comics
Laugh, don't sigh
And dry the last tear from your eye
When my Creator calls from on high
And neither medicine nor pleas apply
Swing on the organ
Sing some happy songs
And dry the last tear from your eye

Swing on the organ
Sing some happy songs
And dry the last tear from your eye.

CHARLOTTE "SISTA C" FERRELL

*Dedicated to the joyful spirit of my Mama, Aljeane Burleson- wife, mother, grandmother, aunt, sister, cousin, and friend - in her Victorious Transition, May 3, 1993. This poem emerged from trying to imagine how to follow her deepest wish that we would not be standing around crying after she was gone. It is a healing poem that Spirit enabled me to present at her **home going** celebration and share with many others.*

Reverb, Revive and Resurge

Reverb
Revive
Resurge
Right here, in front of us
Life has taken on a new plus
Right here, amongst us, a mosaic of earthly treasures surrounds us

Reverberating through the souls of our ancestors
Is a chord ...a note...a prism of possibilities
Harlem Renaissance West Artists revive our culture through their abilities
Their images reveal our heritage like golden threads in a tapestry

Harmonious energy resurges through jazz vibes and tones
It electrifies and socializes eons beyond text on phones
We are elevated to a new walk on life's balance beam
Assuredly, child to elder can achieve Dr. Martin Luther King's dream

Reverb
Revive
Resurge
The time is upon us to re-pattern our walk
Spend time daily in positive thoughts and talk
Life is our canvas, saying "Yes" to Majesty's vision is our tool
Through creativity, all can emerge as a priceless jewel

Now, more than ever, we are assigned to make every life count
We can shift the tide away from clouds of doubt
Through art, movement, music and voices
New intentions can resurge with a bounty of choices

You are the one, we are the ones to:
Reverb
Revive, and
Resurge

Full, Fuller, Fullest

I am full of divine energy.
My heart fully anticipates endless love.
Joy is the order of the day.
This day, this hour, is fuller than this day and hour yesterday.
Tomorrow is not promised but I feel its warmth.
This relaxation into hearing, receiving and submitting to the sublime
Is fulfillment at its fullest!

Chapter 3: Activities
For you with cheer, for your feelings to be held dear

How are you doing?

Are you ready to amplify the cheer in greetings and other communications you give and receive? Are you ready to do a search and replace edit on instances of shallow or subdued communications? Are you ready to be internally cheerful about the messages you give out without any expectations or conditions attached?

In the activities below you will be asked to spend a few minutes reflecting upon ways you feel about yourself, then about a specific person. It is well to be in a comfortable, quiet space, and settle down from any distracting personal activities. Please have a few sheets of paper, index cards or a journal for completing the following activities:

1. Listing- without taking time to judge or measure your words, list ten adjectives that describe how you feel about yourself.

2. Phrasing- without talking to anyone else, write ten phrases that express how you feel about love, itself, not necessarily 'being' in love.

3. Phrasing- without looking at your other lists, write ten phrases that describe how you feel about expressing love to or for any specific person. (Get a mental picture; it could be a child, friend, hero, relative, teacher, and any one).

4. Write a paragraph, or a stanza if a poem that incorporates some of the words and phrases from numbers 1-3, above.

5. Explore how doing these four things made you feel. Which one was easiest? Which was more difficult?

6. Press further, continue with additional paragraphs or stanzas until you have a complete 'product' – a letter, essay or poem. It is not necessary to give this to anyone. Often people with no previous writing experience write incredibly insightful, lovely, joyful, sometimes tearful, poems following this activity at my workshops.

7. Repeat this activity weekly, especially when you are attempting to create a shift in the way you think about or express your feelings.

Chapter 4
For you with hope for your dreams to prosper and float

When designers set about to build a house, they transfer their mental images onto paper. How often do you take time to capture images or feelings from your dreams and transfer them to paper? For some reason, for a very long time, people have been sharing their dreams with me. Maybe it's because I sometimes follow people's hands as they gesture at a space under a table or across the room as they describe where they will be placing things or elements of their dreams. Maybe it's because I am a dreamer. Interestingly, several times a year, friends, students and some family members call to invite me to business openings or share news about dreams that have come into fruition. Regularly offering dream or vision sessions within my classes or meetings has confirmed the value of being a champion for dreams and dreamers. The poems in this chapter encourage dreamers to move forward with courage to nurture and harvest the sweetness, beauty and sense of purpose within their dreams. It concludes with some dream and vision activities that people have enjoyed doing at gatherings or in my classes.

Push Off

Push off – you can sail away
Calm water abounds at the end of the day

Blow your horn – toot your special sound
Time to acknowledge you're anchored on holy ground

Flow away – feel the gentle waves below
Enjoy the feeling of letting your heart glow

Cast off – raise the anchor high
Believe you will succeed if you only try

Sail away – chase the downward cascading sun
Celebrate the course you're off to run

Hope N Joy

Hope is easily said, steadfastly won
The path to hope is woven with patience
Hope looks eternally for its companion, Joy

Joy yielded through a smile or bouncing step
Snatches tendrils of hope wafting by
Joy courts hope like a legendary lover
Woos it till a marriage is born

Hope N. Joy - Joy N. Hope
Welcome to your new home
It is a pleasure to house you
To welcome your visitors and long-term guests
May your windows stay clear so you can beacon all enduring tests

Hope News

We interrupt this broadcast
We interrupt, disrupt, dispute, and commute
this evening's news!

We break into these
tales of doom and words that wound
For a message of hope

We bring you
hope, hope, hope!

From the Southland tonight:
A Latino family is helped from a fire
by five free Masons...

A young African child is pulled safely
from a storm drain by an Asian soccer team...

Three cheers for the Compton High School club
who washed cars all weekend
to save a Mission Row Shelter...

And, news is just in about a retired lady
who prevented a teen mom's suicide
by offering to take care of her child
when she's at work or school

Bring on the news
Bring on the good news
Bring on the message of
Hope, Hope, and Hope News.

Soaring With Recovered Hope and Joy

Soaring with recovered hope and joy
Wouldn't you rather soar than sink?
Soar over problems
Soar past depression and digging into the debilitating past?

Soar into your writing space. Quickly grab a pen
Write about the hope that is lingering in your heart,
Shall I say, "hoping," for a chance to get out?

Recovery from hurt, shock, pain, any serious loss
Is won daily, hourly, sometimes by the minute

Doubt, anxiety, disbelief and fear
Always try to regain a foot hold
Always try to re-secure their positions at the helm of your life

An overflow of joy
Is right there to buoy your hope as you leap over hurdles
Is like cookies in a jar on the top shelf in Grandma's kitchen

Pursuing hope is finding a way to get the cookies out
Without worrying about breaking the jar or her trust,
Know that Grandma set them there, knowing
That from time to time you could use their clout

In Motion

I will put myself in motion
to do those parts of the job
I can do alone
I can catch fish
but I'm terrible at scaling
I can clean house
but I need You to decorate
Catch me up in that motion
of making the things happen
that I've prayed for
Do not let tomorrow catch me here sleeping,
dreaming last year's dreams,
and asking You why
You haven't fulfilled them
Unless I have caught up...
cleaned up
typed up
designed up
glued up
mailed out
phoned out
met about
talked out
prayed out
signed off
All those bits and pieces of little
angel messages,

divine inspirations,
pieces of the puzzle,
That You have given me as the
fabric to build my castle

Treading The Water On Faith

To move from a place of anger, grief and heartache
        takes conscious effort and desire
"Beam me up Scotty," is fine for film and TV
We, who are mortal need help moving from here to there

There *is* such a place as the faith zone.
The faith zone is funny –
        it comes, goes, seems illusive sometimes
It will not go into a frame and be placed on display;
        It needs to flow from your heart daily.
Faith teaches you about itself,
Warms your heart and encourages as you draw near
Leaves you with a chill or aching breast when you pull away

Faith is always at hand, waiting to be invited within
        where it burns like dry mountain bushes
        emits flames to brighten your and others' way
Faith draws what you need to your side

Now I Lay Me Down

Now I lay me down to sleep
I open my eyes and heart to rest
My soul is wonderfully entwined with the Divine
So each hour brings peace sublime

No vile thoughts will my sleep invade
Hearts around me are not enslaved
Rest and renewal are the order of the day.
For this I give thanks as I pray.

YESTERDAY'S POWER TODAY

Yesterday you felt so energized, so full of power and pizzazz
Today you feel nearly flat lined, so devoid of balance and razz-ma-taz

Yesterday you were riding the clouds and sprinting with horses
Today you are lagging behind, barely making it through your courses

Yesterday started with pomp and promise, bright visions for every hour
As the sun tilted toward today the weight of each hour became a burgeoning tower

But up off your memory foam; sleep has done her sweet work
Jump into your prayer zone; know that yesterday was not a quirk
You are on a mission, not propelled by blind ambition
Smell the fumes, grab the mane; get ready to take dreams to a new plane

Yesterday, today, tomorrow all flow in the same stream
Pick your spot; meditate on transforming brown to green
Yesterday, today, tomorrow all flow in the same stream
Plant your feet, open your heart, and release the power of your dreams

Yesterday started with pomp and promise, bright visions for every hour
Today begins the journey toward re-invention and fun, rekindling your power

HARMONY OVER HOLLERING

Announce it from your front door
Announce it from the stairs
Whether you have a stoop or a grandstand
Announce it while you can
    "Love and Peace will abound throughout the land"

The squirrels have a message
The sparrows sense it too
Elements of joy take courage to unearth
Beyond hoarding and scarcity, there is true worth

Open your mouth to sing
Trill down the doubters
Bass and alto have a place with contralto
Sing your song as your mind is inclined to

Strike some new chords
Harmony over hollering
Upbeat patterns presenting new solutions
Unscrew a few bottles and pour libations

Chapter 4: Activities for
"For you with hope for your dreams to prosper and float"

In high school, I disliked and resisted water treading exercises; treed just enough to pass physical education. Now I reflect that with all the unexpected water disasters occurring on our planet, being able to tread water is a basic life preserving skill.

The prospect of burdens being lifted by prayer used to seem as impossible as treading water for ten minutes. Yet, by taking a few minutes to be quiet and enter the "faith zone", I have found my hope continually re-booted or updated. For me, the "faith zone" includes having conversations (a.k.a. prayer) with God and listening, meditating or contemplating what the indwelling spirit is saying. In the "faith zone" things that are trying to worry, discomfort or stress me out pass into other dimensions. I often feel the day's troubles sweep away and flush, as if my bed had a drain. Insights or visions come and I catch them as notes or poetry snippets. While working on this book, I have had to abide in that space more intensely or deeply than others because life has drummed up some startling situations. These include: three unexpected hospitalizations; extreme depletion of my savings and 'retirement' assets; death of two of my closest friends; downsizings occurring within community programs I've loved working with for a decade; having to pack and relocate prior to surgery because my landlord's property went into foreclosure. But the richness of the conversations and contemplation in the faith zone carried me through and the exercises I am sharing have exerted greater confirmation. Reviewing and realizing that intentionally **hopeful words** have power beyond medical prognoses or credit reports I am following my own encouragement to speak boldly about faith.

Typically, Americans are encouraged to submerge their feelings about faith. Have you ever been told that 'faith' isn't a polite subject for mixed company or public conversations? Have you ever felt "odd" or uncomfortable when someone criticizes you for praying or expressing your feelings about faith at work despite knowing your income is backed by dollars that state "IN GOD WE TRUST?"

The following activity invites you to write something that explores or celebrates your comfort level when talking about faith or hope.

1. Journal briefly about an experience where having faith or expressing hope enabled you to accomplish something that seemed impossible or unlikely.

_____

_____

_____

_____

_____

_____

_____

_____

_____

_____

_____

_____

2. Close your eyes and *meditate (remain quiet)* for five to ten minutes. Open yourself to whatever sounds, fragrances, location, images or words come to mind- without drifting off into daydreaming. Use this space, or a notebook, to jot down 10 things you saw and/or felt during this time.

_____

_____

_____

_____

_____

_____

_____

_____

_____

_____

_____

2a. Go back to each note and see if you can identify any connections or patterns. Would you characterize the things you noted as elements of hope, optimism, faith, fear, worry or despair?

3. Increase your boldness in expressing "hope." Listen, attentively to the conversation around your workplace, school, home or gym for 20 to 30 minutes. Note whether the tone and theme evolves more around the things that are going wrong or projected to go wrong, or on the possibilities for success. Notice the succulent temptation to join that flow but resist. Take the scene home and journal about it. Note any two places in the conversation where you could have interjected a hopeful, optimistic comment about the situation. Read, and if you feel comfortable enough, say those things aloud. When you next find yourself the midst of conversation that is whirling, swirling around worst case scenarios, try injecting –not arguing- just interjecting one or two hopeful, optimistic alternative outcomes. Your expression of hope helps others to explore alternative outcomes even when they may not vocalize them.

4. Do this at least once a day, ideally using this book, a small notebook, or journal. This practice will help to evoke a sense of hope while you capture, shape and describe important information regarding your gifts, talents, skills, ideas – or overall life purpose.

Chapter 5

For your encouragement as you pound the pavement

Pavement pounding often means being back at Square One. Many of us have found ourselves there during the shifting sands of our global economy. Pavement pounding is challenging on the feet but is one of those 'load bearing' exercises that helps build strong bones while reducing the risk of osteoporosis. Pavement pounding provides an opportunity for new perspectives about one's neighborhood, community, transportation system and the way we commune with others. Most Californians have grown up with cars as a common or expected part of their life, livelihood or identity. Suddenly people of *means* - teachers, bankers, government workers, event hosts, bookstore owners, auto dealers—are experiencing depletions of savings, retirement accounts, repair 'contingency funds', or subsistence salaries and having to 'hit the pavement.'

Encouragement, faith, cheer and courage are continually needed to endure the silence some 'always hired, never fired' folk are experiencing as they compete with newly graduated, freshly empowered or re-oriented folk, globally. Writing, journaling or poem-making is a definite way to identify and cherish the essence of you... what you bring to the table and the creative concepts you have submerged somewhere within Writing brings clarity. Writing gives you the secret closet or dwelling place where you can safely sort out what you know and love about life and how that can be of service personally and to others. Bringing more value, increasing people's perception of value and identifying places where you can increase the quality of an idea, event, product or service gives you fertile new territory for planting instead of pounding- for sowing seeds that can bring a bountiful new harvest into being. End this chapter by completing the Three "W's" of Encouragement.

- Ways I Encourage others
- Ways people have Encouraged me
- Ways I Encourage myself and the Effect it has upon my efforts

LEFT, RIGHT AND ROUND THE BLOCK

Left, right, keep your feet moving day and night
The pavement is cracked, has places rough and tight
Enough of the *clinkety-clank* typing on keyboards
Your answer is held behind one of these doors
Walk, knock, ring and push
Keep your back straight, your head held high
With all your effort there is one who won't deny
Left, right, round the block and up
You've set your jaw to talk UP
Talk up your skills
Talk up your joy
Talk up your passion
It doesn't matter if all is not in fashion
Pound, push, keep in step
Encourage this one, that one who makes the test
Your turn is coming, may be next
Left, right, right, left, round the corner, up the block
Move with joy, go with grace
Looks like you're pulling into your parking space

A BEING OF LIFE AND LIGHT

I am a being of life and light
Recently discovering the incredible gravity-free zone
In the Zone where no one keeps score
In this Zone my heart soars from practical and predictable
            to indescribable and infinite without definition
Doctors look in their compendiums and draw blanks
No pills, potions, procedures, or protocols are required

In the Zone no one calls *time out*
In this Zone my dreams soar from *as told to stories*
            to visions and missions accomplished
In this Zone my intentions
Launch scripts for movies and conventions
Their meanings and feelings are globally positioned
I am a being of life and light.

CHARLOTTE "SISTA C" FERRELL

CAN YOU RUN WITH THE HORSES?

How can you run with the horses,
      when running with the horsemen tires you out?
Can you run with life's challenges and not grow faint?
Can you stand your ground like a budding saint?
How can you run with the horses,
      when running with the horsemen tires you out?

Sometimes you have to stand and hold your ground
Take pain and suffering without a frown
Come to know that no matter how hard the test
In the end God will help you score the best

How can you run with the horses,
      when running with the horsemen tires you out?
Are you dreaming dreams like the prophets of old?
Are you dreaming dreams like Dr. King, standing with Godly clout?
Have you enlarged your tent or just patched the holes?
Are you standing like Joshua, learning to be courageous and bold?
How can you run with the horses,
      when running with the horsemen tires you out?

Sometimes friends and followers abandon you
Get tired or scared when your vision loses its glow
But when you, from your center, let creativity flow
All that scattered will re-convene when your dreams succeed
Your testimony will confirm that God has blessed beyond sheer need

How can you run with the horses,
      when running with the horsemen tires you out?
Can you see God's power is spread all about?
That you can wait- working on your dreams?
He'll see you trying and help you build your teams.
How can you run with the horses,
      when running with the horsemen tires you out?

Did you know that eagles soar miles above hawks?
They leave ducks in the pond and chickens in their roosts
Relentless mothers stay with their young till they learn to fly
Eagles never allow their eaglets to cling to their nests and cry

Can you, now, out run the horsemen and test the horses?
Can you, now, out run the horsemen and test the horses?
It's your time now - to out run the horsemen and test the horses.
It's our time now - to out run the horsemen and test the horses!

WHEN ALL ELSE FAILS

Take a deep breath
Travel 100 miles in a meaning-steeped minute
Feel the message in a bottle
Examine the corners of the clues

Take hold of hope,
Hold the hope of the ancients, your ancestors, your rock
Anchor your listing boat to a hook of steel

Take a look in the mirror
Hold your eyes in sight
Smile at that amazing, perfect being
Write God a love note with your life.

FIFTEEN PEOPLE JAMMING

Could fifteen people please tell me why we have so many words of wisdom?
Could fifteen people give us a song to ride the waves of time?
Could we try a five-part harmony in two-four time?
                as we swing to the new beat, offbeat nineties?
Nineties logic Nineties manners.
Nineties extended sense of self-indulgence.
Could we have a five-part harmony about the nineties
                as we travel toward Two Thousand Twenty?

Yeah, two thousand and twenty – Twenty Twenty.
Music makes the mood to move ahead, over life's mountains.
Music takes the mad, and mellows it, into water fountains.

Could fifteen people please write some
                music to quiet the neighborly rampage?
Could just One play some saxophone
                to tone down bloody hatred?
Could we have some jammin' sounds
                to move on down life's jagged road?
Could we have some jammin' sounds
                to move on down life's jumbled road?

*This "WordBeat poem" bounced from a studio jam session with Mark Cargill,
Tony Blake, Greg Cook and Bobby Bryant Jr. at CCI, LA. They took my line, "five
part harmony in two-four time," and amazingly made it happen as we recorded
a CD..*

CHARLOTTE "SISTA C" FERRELL

STAVES AND STAKES

Bring them over
There's a party over here
Bring them over
There's a clearing over here
Set in the staves, stake out the sites

Bring them over
There's a garden over here
Bring them over
There are seeds we hold dear
Set in the veggies, stake them up right

Bring them over
There's a rhythm flowing here
Bring them over
There's love soaring here
Set notes in the staves, play them all night

Stave off hunger, stake out abundance
Bring over turnips, tulips and tomatoes
Stave off greed, stake out fair shares
Bring over hope to secure our heirs
Set principles into practice, glow in a new light

Docked and Waiting

There is a gift docked and waiting for you
Did you miss it? Did it slip past?
Shimmering and precious, its twinkling sometimes draws tears
Valued eons beyond the assessor's grasp

The sifting pan cannot hold it
Above and to the North of your sky
Glowing above it holds your image in its eye
You and it are of the same stuff
You and it are of the same stuff formed

Imagined distance has kindred you
Day and night, around the twenty four, it is there
Never disappearing whether or not you stare
Open your eyes, peer beyond the haze

Open your heart, feel its warming love beams
Walk, knowing its force will not let you falter
Loose the sails, reel up the anchor
Undo the ribbons and royally savor the treasure

Scene from the Waiting Room

Rolling down Main Street as Brown, Yellow or multi-colored trucks
Messengers deliver home baked goods, concrete and construction tools
Lifting the crane to cherry pick dangling branches off palm trees

As clerks call out names of clients earnestly hoping to be seen within 15 minutes
Love weaves, alights, touches, brushes and verifies its existence
L.A. County medical center on the inside; Main Street on the outside

Vibrant life intersects urban thoroughfares
Wheels mundanely creak or screech their stories
Moms roll strollers parallel to the sidewalk under construction
Stair-step toddlers tag along behind
A vendor hawks chips, chili, cantaloupe and candy from a converted grocery cart
Appreciative hands and grumbling stomachs pay regardless of the risks

Staff saunter back to 'Reception' after the lunch hour shut down
Eleven forty-five arrivals get slotted for *one fifteen*
Practitioners, waiting beyond, get set to go past *five* again
Names of those waiting for prescriptions get posted, HPPA or not
Hands roll around the clock, etching memories of this scene for the sick or sad

In this and through this, one must pass on
Your need for healing requires a special gown
This scene is temporary, gratitude is more than promissory
Envision the victory as this encounter helps you to empower
Hearts, hands and means to nurture health care like a precious flower

Renewed

Late last night, my body didn't feel right
I considered my past and future plight
I put the phone by the bed last night

As the hours rolled on, I couldn't rest
There were strange flutters in my chest
I put the phone by the bed last night

Early this morning, my back felt a strain
And, my shoulder was racked with pain
I put Spirit in my heart and held tight

When nine passed ten, I got up again
There is painless energy and joy to begin
I will keep Spirit in my heart and hold tight

CHARLOTTE "SISTA C" FERRELL

Chapter 5: Activities
For Your Encouragement

Here are the Three "W's" lists: Spend about 10 minutes thinking about them, then make a list of 5-10 examples under each of the three "Ways" described below.

1.   Ways I encourage others

_____   _____
_____   _____
_____   _____
_____   _____
_____   _____

2.   Ways people have encouraged me:

_____   _____
_____   _____
_____   _____
_____   _____
_____   _____

3.   Ways I encourage myself and the Effect it has upon my efforts

_____   _____
_____   _____
_____   _____
_____   _____
_____   _____

Reflection: After making and comparing these lists, reflect upon whether there is a balance among the "3 W's" or if one of the three is significantly less that the others. Do you see any value in changing this characteristic?

Chapter 6
For your courage as you release fear and turn a new page

For the most part, people don't think it takes courage to release fear. There is a common notion that fear grips us, we freeze, then slowly get our limbs and thoughts circulating about what to do next. We continually hear advertisements that suggest we have separate fears about different things and offer us remedies to help us get over our fear of...flying, speaking, bullying, swimming, etcetera. During his first Inaugural address in 1933, Franklin Delano Roosevelt appealed to Americans to shake their fear of a worsening economy when he asserted, "The only thing we have to fear is fear itself." Coming from a man who won the highest office in the land while wheel-chair bound from polio, this sentiment seemed to call for a leap of faith. Historical commentators have

CHARLOTTE "SISTA C" FERRELL

since noted that he was paving the way to acceptance of the New Deal - the largest infusion of government money (then) ever focused on social issues. John Buescher, a historian and former Voice of America broadcaster, notes that the fear slogan predated F.D.R and was published in a 1928 booklet, *The Power of* Concentration, by William Walker under the pen name, Theron Q. Dumont. He wrote:

> *There is no justification for the loss of courage. The evils by which you will almost certainly be overwhelmed without it are far greater than those which courage will help you to meet and overcome. Right, then, must be the moralist who says that* **the only thing to fear is fear.**

Throughout his classic ***Dune*** series of science fiction books, Frank Herbert weaves the mythical *Benet Gisserit* litany *against fear*:

> *I must not fear. Fear is the mind-killer. Fear is the little-death that brings total obliteration. I will face my fear. I will permit it to pass over me and through me. And when it has gone past I will turn the inner eye to see its path. Where the fear has gone there will be nothing. Only I will remain.*

On a personal level, I know that when I let fear creep into my life, it disrupts my sleep. It has caused chest pain so severe I thought I was having a heart attack. From the lips of a cardiologist to the writings of thought leaders, the impetus to be courageous enough to confront fear itself has taken root and borne fruit. In a small book, *The Miracle of Mindfulness*, Thich Nhat Hahn shares stories and a few simple practices that can give monumental relief from stress, fear and anxiety. Chief among these practices are meditation and "mindfulness." When I read his challenge to the widely expressed value of multitasking, I had to press pause on the internal arguments button. Hahn makes a convincing argument that multi-tasking generates fear about *dropping the ball* or missing something important. *Mindfulness* encourages you to be present with whatever you are doing and grateful for the people or things that enable you to enjoy any aspect of life.

I wrote the poems in this chapter while practicing the 'mindfulness' of being at one with the thoughts or words that wanted to emerge. Not writing while eating, not writing with the TV or music providing background sounds (aka distractions). Just being courageous enough to let what wanted to emerge come forward without worrying about how others would interpret or receive my sentiments. What about you? Are you ready to insulate your mind and heart from fear storms? Check out the poems and the activities for this chapter.

CHARLOTTE "SISTA C" FERRELL

DOCKED AND WAITING

There is a gift docked and waiting for you
Did you miss it? Did it slip past?
Shimmering and precious,
Its twinkling sometimes draws tears
Valued eons beyond the assessor's grasp

The sifting pan cannot hold it
Above and to the North of your sky
Glowing above, something holds your image in its eye
You and it are of the same stuff formed

Imagined distance has kindred you
Day and night, around the twenty-four, it is there
Never disappearing whether or not you stare
Open your eyes, peer beyond the haze

Open your heart, feel its warming love beams
Walk, knowing its force will not let you falter
Loose the sails, reel up the anchor
Undo the ribbons and royally savor the treasure

There is a gift docked and waiting for you.

STOMPING IT OUT

One foot down, one foot up
One foot ahead, one foot planted solidly behind
Pausing long enough to feel the easing of pressure
The loosing, lightening of the load of un-forgiveness

One foot down, one foot up
The ugliness of the exchange, buried
One foot ahead, one foot planted solidly behind
Observing tender new shoots emerging along the sidelines
The bustling, bursting forth of tulip petals from buds

One foot down, one foot up
Feel the rush of fresh air rooting out stagnant bitter thoughts
One foot ahead, one foot ready to spring from behind
Enjoying vibrant greens, purples and magentas rolling into view
Jump-starting your jubilant, unfettered dance across dimensions

One foot down, one foot up
Hear the rush of glad tidings one second after the old door closes
Feel the welcoming hands giving five and love pats on the back
Two feet jumping in the air with jubilation
Reaping the benefits of the 'get out of jail free' card
Breathing the rarified air of a new start

CHARLOTTE "SISTA C" FERRELL

COLLARD TENACITY

Give me the tenacity of a crisp collard
Let my ebony richness magnify its verdant green
As I reach out my hand, give me tough veins
Able to circulate life-giving nourishment
To the generations yet as seedlings

With each year, let me lay down new roots
Roots ready to supplement the meager fare
Of loveless harshness some societies secrete
As they admonish others to "be satisfied"

Enable my leaves to secure safe harbor
For the many remanded to sleep on the streets
Make me an agent of harvesting the best from our past
Give me the courage to motivate all to shoulder
Their part in laying a new garden of hope and happiness

But if our caviar and candlelight cousins, siblings or neighbors
Refuse to set an extra plate while tossing garbage daily
Let me regularly be ready to serve savory collards and cornbread
And never forget to till and plant for the next harvest

Renewed

Late last night, my body didn't feel right
I considered my past and future plight
I put the phone by the bed last night

As the hours rolled on, I couldn't rest
There were strange flutters in my chest
I put the phone by the bed last night

Early this morning, my back felt a strain
And my shoulder was racked with pain
I located the Spirit within and held tight

When ten passed nine, I got up again
I found painless energy and joy to begin
I will keep Spirit in my heart and hold tight
I will greet each day with total delight

MOTHER STRONG ... MOTHER SOFT

Mother strong in life embracing
Little loves' legs and feet
Giving light from dawn to dusk

Mother strong in life proclaiming
Little rules for life's upbringing
Quoting chapter, verse of scripture
Hoping fertile seeds will follow.

Mother strong in life rejoicing
Pillows of love and laughter singing
Cuddles, cuddles, chauffeured cars
Hoping all will child not spoil.

Mother turning life unbending
Little twinges, steps that falter
Some days soaring others dwindling
Wondering if all is worth the kindling.

Mother soft in life unraveling
Seeds she sowed gathering, searching
Probing tendrils wrapping around her
Confirming that their paths will praise her.

WORD PATCHER

You are the one
The one who doesn't skip over cracks in the pavement
The one who brings asphalt with sparkle dust
To give unincorporated zones that Hollywood feel

You are the one
The one who looks at pin-pricked walls and removes spare tacks
The one who brings spackle and wood glue
To give beleaguered dwellings that *Extreme Makeover* feel

You are the one
The one who hears words and hot retorts bouncing off the ceiling
The one who brings word patches with soothing tones
To give threadbare relationships that *Enchanted Garden* feeling

You are the one
The Wall Patcher
The Road Patcher
The Word Patcher
The Urban Village Healer among us

CHARLOTTE "SISTA C" FERRELL

NEW LIFE

Oops
I felt it
A little fluttering, bumping evidence of new life

I am pregnant. Pregnant again. At MY age?
You have planted a seed that has taken root in the chambers of my heart.
It was hiding there
Dividing and budding and budding and dividing
I thought I had strong prophylactics wrapped around it
But ...some greater power found an unshielded corner

I said, go away.
But you smiled in emerald silence.
You, immune to doubt,
Kept moving, kept swaying, kept a vigil.
When I thought all was dry, barren and healed over with scar tissue,
When I would have kept smiling and discarding cards offered from various hands,
You slipped the ace of hearts into the deck.

And it grew... amazingly it grew to a royal flush
How does this happen, this rounding, mounding pregnancy of the heart?
How does the sun shine?
The oceans flow?
Only through divine will.
I am welcoming this divine blessing
It is a baby I will not abort.

I have no comparison for this moment.
There is a feeling long since passed... gone.
Doubts have been dashed – can I parent, be a guardian, mother such a being?
It is unmistakably your courageous life, your essence, your seed that is growing.
With you, I do not long or hunger for food after dining
My sleep is peaceful and refreshed
Gone are days of waking up wishing to re-enter the bed

I love this little one growing in my heart
I can barely imagine the incredible joy
Of feeling it enlarge as it asserts its new life.

Chapter 6: Activities

"For your courage as you release fear and turn a new page"

What about you? Have you considered any ways that fear is causing you to postpone, negate or take refuge from the idea of turning a new page? Explore these activities along or with a partner.

1. Take a quick 5 minutes and make a list of five things you resolved or set an intention to achieve last year. Leave 5 lines after each one.
2. On the first line after each item, simply write whether you achieved that "thing "or not.
3. In the remaining space briefly ponder/explore whether or not fear was a factor in your not accomplishing that thing.

Now if you are working with a partner, or doing this as part of a small group, this is a great place to stop and have a brief discussion about taking on the courage to face down the fear or fears that kept you from accomplishing those things.

4. If you are doing this activity alone, sit still for a few minutes and reflect on the size and beauty of your intention compared with the paltry, smallness of the fear that kept you from achieving it. Write an affirmation to accomplish it this year.
5. Put your fear into a funny poem and bounce it until you are laughing out loud.

Chapter 7
For you with hugs and smiles right here or across the miles

How do hugs make you feel? Virginia Satir, a multiple honorary Ph.D. awardee and family therapist is often quoted for saying, *"We need four hugs a day for survival, eight for maintenance and twelve for growth."*

While it may not always be possible for us to give or receive that many physical hugs daily, it is entirely possible to send words that give a 'fresh-hugged' feeling. If you have ever had a bunch of angry or mean words hurled at you, you know they can sting like darts. Sometimes those stings linger and nudge you toward a bad response or grumpy mood. But, with a few tweaks in attitude, you can bring up your duck feathers and let them roll off your back. Have you ever witnessed the beauty of two family members who haven't spoken for years embracing each other until one or both break into a smile? I've witnessed that same response when a child gives a parent a poem, or I've turned a challenging situation into cherished words. Poems can present themselves as duck feathers that not only shield a soft underbody, they also they can also stimulate the warm satisfied feeling associated with hugging.

I enjoy hosting and participating in spoken word events for adults and kids. Listening to people share authentic, heart-felt, sincere words of hope, joy, love, peace, freedom and justice generates a positive vibration that I've witnessed sweetening temperaments and facial expressions. Sometimes hugging someone with sincere, pertinent words shocks them into reflecting upon the nastiness of something they have said. Not all hugs are alike. Sometimes physical or 'word hugs' are so powerfully extended they seem to put you in a different orbit. Sometimes hugs are like the coating on *M&Ms, you can get them to release their sweetness quickly or slowly according to whether you crunch or savor them.*

Poems can be printed or special paper or sent by text. While texting is sometimes a platform for inane insults, it provides an overwhelmingly greater opportunity to exchange poetic hugs throughout the day. Writing a poem takes a little time, but even if is **just for you**, hug yourself happy with some worry-free, succulent words. I'd love to hear what you think after reading my hug-inspired poems.

Mmmm. Do YOU?

Mmmm. Do you smell it?
It's like cherry blossoms blowing in the wind
It's like night shade musky when night begins

Shhh. Do you hear it?
It's like weeping willows rustling by the lake
It's like humming birds giving leaves a little shake

Now. Do you feel it?
Something inside is beginning to quake
Something inside is causing the fever to break

Now. Do you know it?
Nerves and neurons are finding new paths
Nerves on edge are losing tension and wrath

Mmmm. Do you smell it?
It's like fresh cookies straight from the oven.
It's like fresh rain falling straight from heaven.

Shhh. Do you hear it?
Flame boiled hope is building up steam.
Love is rustling, waking from a dream.

Now. Do you know it?
Joy is singing and saying hello.
Joy is dancing and making our faces glow.

CHARLOTTE "SISTA C" FERRELL

Now. Do you know it?
Love has come on stage between curtain calls.
Love has come anew bringing summer in the fall.

An Evening Word Snifter

Hmmm

Into the base of life's diamond crystal goblet

Pours the sentiments and sediment of the day

The essence of things completed with excellence weaves through the room.

A sultry hint of honey tingles the taste buds

While a lemony kiss calms nerves and tendons

Trailing wisps of liberally-shared, kindly-worded compliments warm the throat

Swirling downward, simmering columns of joy take root in the heart,

Birthing moments of quiet reflection, satisfaction for the effort spent

Ummm

Back to the lips it comes once more to seal happiness with a kiss

In the exchange receiving a seal of *happy U-ness*

From clasped hands to hands resting in peace

The Word Snifter empties willingly,

Waiting to deliver a sensational tomorrow

CHARLOTTE "SISTA C" FERRELL

BAKE UP A BATCH OF COOKIES TODAY

Bake up a batch of cookies today
Go ahead and make somebody's day
To the wheat, cut off at the bend,
               cracked, racked, ground into flour
Add fresh butter creamed with brown sugar
Stir in some raisins and cinnamon for flavor

Bake up a Batch of Cookies Today
Go ahead and make somebody's day
Roll out some dough
Shape hearts and get the gingerbread men in order
Brush on a little glaze
Insert red hot eyes that diminish the haze

Bake up a batch of cookies today
Go ahead and make somebody's day
Transform tears to twinkles with chocolate chips
Warm frozen smiles with oatmeal hermits
Shift the balance with peanut butter crisps

Bake up a batch of cookies today
Go ahead and make somebody's day

TWELVE HUGS A DAY

Twelve hugs a day are what some say you need for happiness
Would that be three for breakfast, three for lunch, and three for dinner?
And two fitted in as 'between meal' snacks?

Or, would that be two as you leave home,
Four when you get where you're going,
Four as you go through the day greeting and meeting,
And two as you work your way back in?

Maybe that would be four saying good bye from point A
Two as you arrive at point B,
Three as you go from a mixer at C to dinner at D,
And three as you wind your way back to A!

Twelve hugs a day
Twelve the hard or easy way
Twelve given sincerely
Twelve received tenderly
Exchanging a breath of blessings
As you part and go on your way

I AM YOUR MOTHER

I am here as you traverse the ridges beyond your common ground
I am here with words of encouragement and reams of nylon
I am here to cheer you or catch you as the winds wisp or rage
I am your mother

I am here as you break free of tea parties, tutors and tennis matches
I am here with touch screens, touch tones and healing touch
I am here to coach you or celebrate your successes
I am your mother

I am here for the pin pricks and pinched nerves along your path
I am here with a magnifying glass and glue as you break the cocoon
I am here with salve for a hundred feet before you take flight
I am your mother

I am here with hope while others shout, "Give up."
I am here with one more recipe for potatoes and onions
I am here with spices and drops of sesame oil, or almond essence
I am your mother

Do Something Different

I put my soul on ice
And I went somewhere un-nice
Long about a year or two
But I'm all right now
I'm going to do something different
Do something different right now
I'm going to do something different
right about now

Maybe I'll do something different
While I'm recording with you
Run my voice from brain to spine,
Create shifts in your mind.
Hug away anything unkind.

Maybe I'll burn all the wax
Disrupt the digital tracks
Or just twist your hair
Like wool blowing in the air
Yesterday I was unable to relax

But I'm going to do something different right now
I 'm going to do something different
right about now
Take a word you've rarely heard
Shape and make it sing like a bird
I'm going to do something different right now.

CHARLOTTE "SISTA C" FERRELL

Can you do something different right now?
Has your soul grown too cold to learn how?
Can you break down brass tacks?
Embrace life with a whole new act?
Can you do something different right now?
Can you do something different,
Right about now?

Chapter 8

For you with wishes and more as you open that new door

We launch a lifetime of door-opening experiences the first time we rise on our tip toes, turn a knob and feel a door swing open. Sometimes it is the door to a new bedroom, school, car, office or home; sometimes it is to a hospital or convalescent room. Sometimes it is the door to your mind. When you wish upon a poem it finds your way to your heart, hand and mouth. Make a wish, internalize a prayer. Open the door and see what visions emerge to greet you.

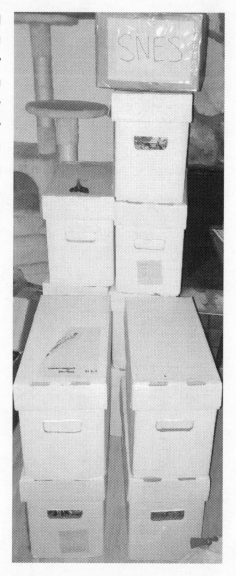

CHARLOTTE "SISTA C" FERRELL

FEEL IT

Feel it - glance left, glance right,
Touch lightly at the bridge of your hand
Can you feel it?
Is there a pulse still?

Break the barrier to the dreams
Pulsing lightly in the center of your heart
Pop some popcorn, notice the sound
Kernels pulsing to life with the oil and heat
Can you hear them working their charm?

Savor the silence, mute the background
Notice the pattern of your heart beat
Does it surge? Does it thump?
How does it pulse in a storm?

Feel it - greet it, seek its solace
Savor its simplicity
Salute its majesty hidden within
Can you find love there for a friend?

WHAT IF You...?

Into the debriefing pits you proffer and flow
Words, phrases, statements of what could have been
"This would go better with that,"
"That would be better with this"
You wax eloquent without end

To the event post mortems, you write and bring
Reviews and assessments of all you have seen
"This would be more efficient than that"
"That would be more efficient than this"
You write tombs until the ink grows thin

To the brainstorming table you search and blow
Fog, and *devil's advocate-ism* into ideas you ream
What if this instead of *why not that*
Why *that won't work* instead of *what about this*
You ponder and puzzle until sessions end

Into your journal you expound and explain
Visions, dreams and beauty from another scene
What if you did *these* instead of dissecting *those?*
What if you ignited *these* and implemented *those?*
What if you closed the craters and birthed your dreams?
What if you served cake with strawberries and cream?

What if you...?

How Are You with Mama, Mom, and Momma?

From behind walls they write:
Dear Mama, Dear Mom, Dear Momma
I wish I had... if only I had...
I'm sorry you have to ... I promise someday I will...

From tables behind bars
Through censor readers' hands
They write:
>   I love you Mama
>   Luv' you Mom
>   Always love you Momma

"Please" abounds through
Hard bodies with broken hearts
Chiseled faces with choked back tears
Clenched teeth confessing yearnings of the heart
To see the eyes, feel the reassurance
>   Of Mama's love
>   Of Mom's forgiveness
>   Of Momma's reassurance

What about you, with
Freedom under your feet and by your side
How are you heeding Mama's advice?
How are you expressing Mom's love?
How are you welcoming Momma's wisdom?
How are you reflecting Mama, Mom, and Momma?

I have done poetry workshops or 'spoken word' at several correctional facilities. I was invited to do a workshop at a maximum security youth facility during a California Red Ribbon Week which is focused around substance abuse prevention. I shared poems dealing with family and social issues. When I asked the young men to write a 5-line poem reflecting what they got out of the workshop; more than 25 wrote long poems (15+ lines) expressing feelings of love; regret, desire for forgiveness and hope for new futures with regard to their mothers. What if more boys were encouraged to share their sentiments earlier?

Heart of My Heart – a jazz poem

Heart of my heart
Are you there? Are you at home?
Heart, have you gone deaf?
Can't you hear his feelings groan?

Heart of my heart
Something's gone wrong.
You beat and repeat,
But you're home all alone.

Heart of my heart
I think you're tone deaf
Music's playing. Everyone's dancing
But your feet are both left.

Heart of my heart
Have you anything in store?
Dinner's served. Only half have eaten
But the kitchen holds no more.

Heart of my heart
What of passion and power?
The light switches are on,
But its been dark for over an hour.

Heart of my heart
For the love of God, wake up!
Time's flying. People are dying

You have got to rev up.

Heart of my heart
Come out of your shell
The war's over. Shooting's stopped.
Can't you even tell?

Heart of My Heart

Heart of my heart,
Come fly another way
The stars are bright.
Let's let the night
Lead us into a new day
Heart of my heart
Don't wither with despair
We are but one, let's chase the sun
And just soar through the air

Chapter 8: Activities
"For you with wishes and more as you open that new door"

A popular commercial asks, "What's in your wallet?" What comes to mind when you think about a new door you are facing in life? What do you have to work with when a friend calls to express their doubt or anxiety about "new door" issues, such as changing their hair color, relationship, or job?

Wallet-building Activity #1: Fold a sheet of paper in half. Set your timer for five minutes. On the left side of the paper make a list of judgmental, evaluative words. Set your timer for another five minutes. On the right side make a list of probing, encouraging, exploratory words.

Reflection: How many words did you develop on the two sides of the paper given the same time period?

Wallet-building Activity #2: Picture a new door (life situation) you may be facing right not. Take five minutes and switch each of your judgmental, evaluative, anxious words into a positive, energizing, encouraging or exploratory word.

Application- Write a five to 10-line poem about opening your new door using the words you listed in Wallet-building activity #2.

Chapter 9
For your peace as you take in all life has to teach

Life for humans begins with a fierce competition of which microscopic union will emerge as a vibrant multi-celled, multi-faceted being. Our lives mirror the months where some days are calm, while others are filled with unexpected bumps, thumps, swirls, and squeezes. Having faith, asserting affirmations, or pursuing a purpose, makes life easier. But, these things don't prevent us from encountering life's potholes, pitfalls or pain. Words have the power to rage against storms or welcome the rainbow and the return of calmness. Even when you feel most hopeless, one fruitful practice is to 'speak those things that are not as if they were.' I used to be much more volatile; occasionally I still am. However, the faster I shut my mouth, open myself to envisioning 'peace', and begin writing, the sooner I feel more peaceful.

Writing is not a rabbit's foot, but I have found that of all the kinds of writing I do, writing poetry provides the most insight and peace. I am not a fan of poetry/spoken word gatherings where people smash each other's eardrums or sensibilities with profane, hateful, angry poetry. That has a home in poetry therapy sessions (which I have co-facilitated with a psychologist). From L.A. to Toronto, and among various age groups, I have witnessed the peace-sharing, peace-empowering effects of writing, speaking, and even watching moving poetry. Heart Balm activities help move words from hidden, rough internal crevices to paper, recordings and images where they can be explored, nurtured and re-imagined. Uncovered and re-imagined, they can reveal the hidden piece of the puzzle. It doesn't matter whether or not your words rhyme, it is more important to give yourself permission to take thoughts and let them float. Explore the balm of 'putting pen to paper' or 'fingers to keyboard' and just see what "something within" wants to share with you. I wish you peace as you explore how your marvelous life journey unfolds as poetry and prose.

MELTDOWN TO MOUNTAINS

Have you ever melted down?
Felt your eyes hit tilt and feel like they were going to burst?

Have you ever felt your bones overheat like they would burn up?
Felt your blood rush like water through a dam?

Have you ever had to hum one of Grandma's old songs?
While counting to a million by hundreds
While your hands wanted to choke or punch?
Have you ever felt your resolve slipping away, edging out of touch?

Have you ever felt wisps of angel drawn breath?
Clearing your eyes and cooling your steamy forehead,
Re-balancing your heartbeat,
Settling your warring nerves?

Have you ever felt the exhilaration,
Enjoyed the buoyant reverberation of escaping the boiler room
And finding a cool drink?

Meltdowns can leave messy, sticky, puddles
Or, like taffy, they can be pulled into shape
Put back in balance before they
       Break up a relationship
       Dissolve a dream
       Or demolish a reputation

Look up, look within, you have power to expend

CHARLOTTE "SISTA C" FERRELL

Draw on eons of examples

Peaceful responses paving highways through mountains

Heat forging gold into goblets

Forgiveness Councils reshaping war parties

Seconds save with CPR

Salicylic acid stalls the pinball path of clots

Breathing, counting, open-eyed praying

Tames riptides to wading pools

Now I Lay Me Down

Now I lay me down to sleep
I open my eyes and heart to rest
My soul is with the Divine, aligned
Hour by hour I grow more inspired

Now villains, no vile forces will my sleep invade
Hearts around me are not enslaved
Rest and renewal are the order of the day
For these precious things I give thanks as I pray

CHARLOTTE "SISTA C" FERRELL

WELCOMING DARKNESS

Darkness bit the dust
Lingered along the edges
Before easing into the folds,
Darkness danced with the sun

Darkness enveloped the lovers
Dancing to *No Woman No Cry*
Brushed new hope into their eyes
Caressed the dust and bid goodbye

Darkness wove golden threads with fuchsia
Splashed the sea and electrified navy waves
Gave photographers and seagulls a treat
Colored affirmations and meditations

Darkness is a nightly gift
Inviting relaxation, rejuvenation
Welcoming a descent into new dimensions
Welcoming new thoughts to greet the sun

Seven Times Seven

Seven times Seven
Warnings - endlessly given
Un-forgiveness ends live and joy

Seven times Seven
Friends, brothers, sisters
All professing belief
Need the relief of a forgiving exchange

Truly denominations and divisions
Can by hardened hearts be imprisoned
Seven times Seven, or maybe Seventy
Keeping count is expressed as profanity

Seven times Seven
Sacred texts profess and repeat
Messages dreamed, spoken, written
Un-heralded lead to a bitter end
Life without grace, hanging on a slender thread

Seven times Seven
You can come from a different bag
You have faces and occasions to tag
Using care and ingenuity
You can re-spin situations so everyone wins

Bones Board Themselves

Boarded bones board themselves
Down flat, hard on the table
Oops- a mistaken piece lifted up
Fists bang, voices rise
Boarded bones board themselves

Boarded words board themselves
Unanswered questions hit the board
Words attempted to be regrouped, re-patterned
Bring anger, disquiet, discredit
Boarded lies board themselves

Slap, bang, fast rack up of 5, 10, 15 points
How many points does a little lie earn?
How many does one subtract?
Board room to board room
Bedroom to bedroom
House to house
Boarded lies board themselves

A little sweetness, a little padding
Two words to the left, toggle a little to the right
Two clicks of the mouse
One folded paper note in a bag
Sacred lessons mixed with coded love notes
Boarded lies board themselves

Rise and fly
Fly and drop like buzzard leavings
Dismissed from the table, dismissed from the boudoir
Dismissed by the doctor, dismissed by the deacon

A partnership cannot withstand threes for fives
Multiples of six and nine earn no score
Boarded lies board themselves
Boarded lies once exposed
Bear fruit no more
Rise and fly, this game is closed to rule-thrashers

A "action poem" can assuage even the disappointment of discovering that sometimes people who profess to be proponents of good can be more like Gotham City characters.

PATIENCE THROUGH 3000 PIECES

Patience, "Don't throw that piece away."
Patience it is truly intriguing
There is a pattern, there is a message
In the way the three thousand connect

Look at the shades at the center
See the groves and similar curves
Find the ones with double notches
Somewhere there are double grooves

Life never jumps from two to twenty
Between fifteen and fifty there are bends aplenty
Sometimes they merge at forty and sixty
It takes patience to discern the ways

Much is learned from piece three to three thousand
Getting a steady table, off the beaten path, for one
Cooperation and collaboration with the curious
Short-circuits frustrating breaks and falls

Patience through three thousand pieces
Brings lessons to share and laugh over
Creates a pace and nurtures peace
Want to join me at the puzzle store?

THE ATTITUDE FOR LATITUDE

The point
The precise point at the end of your arm
Is less geometry than internal chemistry.
The mileage that comes from the smile on your face
Grants you passage and secures your lifelong space

Gaining the attitude for latitude can exist at any altitude
Cribs to trikes; bikes to buses; stretch limos to seven fifty sevens
Ascending, descending, transcending lines
Have their places on laminated maps
Your passion, your ascension keeps others from floating adrift

The point
The precise point in your transition from mundane to Meister
Is less geography than internal combustion
Confusion exited stage left with the gloom
Leading roles and crafting courses
Are the simple order of the day

The precise point at which everything seemed to fall apart
Was the ascension station
The jettison point
When foiled plans met with unexpected goodness
New formulas emerged from the fragile threads

There goes the Gift-Meister

There you go
Giving, gifting, generating joy
On your way
Throughout the day
Your royal mission to deploy

There you go
Just in the nick of time
Writing away tears,
Taking a stand to reverse fears.
Gracefully generous, of grateful living you remind

There you go
The anticipated, welcomed friend
Generating ideas and energy
Igniting hearts amidst winter winds
Cherishing all you can do before day's end
There you go

Chapter 9: Activities
"For your peace as you take in all life has to teach"

The middle of the morning is the typical time that life's issues love to storm across your bed, couch or computer console. Just as you are trying to settle into sleep, here comes the circus. Or, right in the middle of a conversation at a gathering, someone decides to zing you with a joke and 'oops', there goes the tilt button. The world has thousands of bodies of water that peacefully flow along, making a home for plants, people and animals, most of the time. But sometimes they overflow, swirl and storm carrying lessons and miracles in their path. Here are some "less travelled" pathways to peace. I've explored them with groups. Let me know how they work for you alone or with a friend.

Get to the Bottom of Things
A. Check out your Feet – a personal care activity. Often we repeat or receive blessings "from the tops of our heads to the soles of our feet." Did you know there are nerves in your feet that connect with every part of your body?

1. When was the last time you looked at the soles of your feet? Whether you are lying down, or sitting in a chair, cross your leg and alternately look at the bottom of each foot. Rub it. Put some lotion on it and massage it. Massage each toe and allow yourself to think about all the places your feet have taken you.
   a. Reflection: Are your feet clean or dirty; are they dry and cracked, or moist and smooth? How do your toenails feel?
   b. Take a few minutes to journal about this. How did rubbing the soles of your feet make you feel? Is there any comparison or similarity in the way you are treating your feet and the way you feel 'life' is treating you? Did massaging your feet help you relax?

2. Check out your Mind – Curtis Mayfield gave us a powerful clue to finding peace when he sang, "Check out your mind, it's been with you all the time." Professional trainers have athletes repeat certain twists, lifts, sweeps and strokes hundreds of times in order to have their muscles perform the moves instantly and effortlessly when needed.

    a. Reflection: What are your bouncing and reverbing through your mind?

    b. Take a few minutes to journal a page about this.

    c. Using the poem-making activities from chapter two, try your hand at writing your own mind-clearing peace poem.

3. Check out your Heart – Launched in 1937, an old time, crime-fighting, radio program started each show with the question, "Who *knows what evil lurks in the hearts of men?*" and the answer was, "the Shadow". On the other side of the spectrum, sages, scientists and spiritual leaders have professed that peace and anger cannot dwell in people's hearts simultaneously. Numerous mental conditions have been ascribed to people who act as if they can. Check out your heart:*

    a. Reflection – When someone cuts you off on the road, takes a parking space you were waiting on, or accidentally spills something on you, what is your anger-o-meter on a scale of 1-10, with 10 being the angriest. Are you able to call to memory the words of a song like Pharrell's "Happy", or a phrase like, "Peace be still?"

    b. Heart-healthy journaling: In your journal, create a space or area for writing a daily note of gratitude for a minimum of five days. Whatever your most pressing life issue is for that day, attempt to find some aspect of gratitude about it.

    c. *Poetic pondering – O.k. you're getting the hang of this. Write a 5-1- line peace poem of your own or use any one of mine as a pattern where you change the words to suit your situation.*

Chapter 10
For your health as you bask in excellent health

How are you? Now quick before you answer, think and state exactly how you'd like to feel. Are you living through your symptoms, dragging your diagnoses from checkup rooms to cocktail parties or conference rooms? It takes a real transformation to consistently speak of, or celebrate, excellent health. People sometimes give you a funny look when you answer, "Perfect, or excellent." In this chapter, I am sharing some poems of joy from my "best days" along with those written when I had to trade doctors' dire prognoses for the promise of God's grace.

Poetry and journaling are potent forms of health writing. They enable you to embrace the fragility and majesty of being a human being. Health writing is a way of achieving and celebrating perfection while being deigned imperfect by traditional medical measuring devices. To me, perfection is an attribute of peace that enables expressions of love, hope and joy over anguish and despair. Health writing also enables and elicits authentic expressions during the times you feel frustrated, abandoned and disgruntled. Being able to identify these emotions then paint, write, film or otherwise acknowledge them gives you a template for setting goals and re-imagining or re-visioning those feelings. Finding a poem written by someone else, or writing one to share, definitely communicates the vision of basking in excellent health.

Poems, for me, are often a shoulder to cry on when everyone else is asleep or not ready to hear *stuff* I sometimes need to release. They are the blessing in the storm - the winds that take me up the mountain and into the clouds. They are a vehicle for "crying out loud" and expressing gratitude to God, and fellow life-travelers. They are a basin to wash away tears and revive your feet.

When I wrote my first book, ***From Pillows to Pillars***, I thought poetry was something to do while waiting for hopes, prayers and dreams to be answered. Now I know poems as my "transformers" - vehicles of hope, and testimony-bearers. During the metamorphosis from being a coffee house poet to someone who lets the creative arts drive my teaching, speaking and writing, I called what I do, "Heart Clearing ~ Heart Writing." Now, I call it Heart Balm. Using Heart Balm for workshops and individual healing sessions, has generated immense joy and lightness as people find and expel their hidden pockets of un-forgiveness, disappointment or despair through journaling, writing poems, and crafting stories.

Skipping and Smiling

Skip, Skip, Skip
My heart is so happy it feels like it is skipping a beat
I'm afraid to go to work today
They may think I am all play or dazed by the heat
They may mistake my floating mood with substances untrue
Would not understand what faith has imbued
To get up fluidly, feeling my back and buttocks flow with my brain
Without muscles complaining or sending spasmodic pain
As they did unpredictably in a time sooner recalled than not

Now, there is room for daily celebration
In faith I proclaimed what I had been told
>   *If you want it, speak it*
>   *Bring it from the heavenly realm*
>   *Bring it from another dimension*
>   *Call it in, speak it up*
Too simple I thought, there must be more
Candles, crosses, float tanks, a three-day fast
But none of these are set in stone
As miracles go, the first may be last

I cried and I tried to imagine with all my heart
What it would be like to get up with
No doubt or depression holding me fast to my seat
Now I am skipping and smiling. My director thinks I'm in love
Someone suggested maybe I should take a sample
To the test room floors above

But there's no substance to confuse this comfort I am feeling
It is God's grace and blessings
Upon the situations with which I've been dealing

Utt oh, Utt oh Spirit Loves You, I Do Too

A song poem recorded with drums, flute and tambourine

Utt oh, utt oh	I've got my health back
Utt oh, utt oh	My life is back on track
Utt oh, utt oh	I've got my strength back
Utt oh, utt oh	No pain is in my back
Utt oh, utt oh	Doctors' bad news lost again
Utt oh, utt oh	Because Spirit is my friend
Utt oh, utt oh	I've got complete joy
Utt oh, utt oh	I'm floating like a toy
Utt oh, utt oh	I've got my life back
Utt oh, utt oh	My spirit is Intact
Utt oh, utt oh	I see the sun RISE
Utt oh, utt oh	My eyes are On the Prize
Utt oh, utt oh	My Lord is my best friend
Utt oh, utt oh	He's with me thick and thin
Utt oh, utt oh	No worry will be spent
Utt oh, utt oh	My body's a hundred percent
Utt oh, utt oh	I really love my life
Utt oh, utt oh	It's full of joy, not strife
Utt oh, utt oh	My friends know this is true
Utt oh, utt oh	Spirit loves you, I do too
Utt oh, utt oh	Spirit loves you, I do too

CHARLOTTE "SISTA C" FERRELL

Utt oh, utt oh   Spirit loves you, I do too

This poem emerged one Sunday morning in 2006 after a week of being housebound with 'hellacious" pain. As I bounded up from the bed, I said "utt-oh", and the poem was on.

A BEING OF LIFE AND LIGHT

I am a being of life and light
Recently discovering the incredible gravity-free zone
In the Zone where no one keeps score
In this Zone my heart soars from practical and predictable
To indescribable and infinite without definition
Doctors look in their compendiums and draw blanks
No pills, potions, procedures, or protocols required

In the Zone no one calls *time out*
In this Zone my dreams soar from *as told to stories*
To visions and missions accomplished
Launching scripts for box office door crashers

CHARLOTTE "SISTA C" FERRELL

From BOGO to BO-I-GO

When the jingle in your pockets jangles on E
When the sight of "sale" signs threaten to bring misery
When you don't have the first something to make BOGO work
It is the perfect time to give all gloomy emotions a jerk
Time to flip the switch from BOGO to BO-I-GO

Let not your heart be heavy or your spirit, sad
BO-I-GO is more available than Seven-Elevens
BO-I-GO is more lavish than stretch limos for stars
BO-I-GO. Be One in God's Omnipresence.
BO-I-GO. Be Outstanding in God's Omni-power

SMOOTHING THE EDGES

Red to orange to blue to white hot
Pain shooting, chomping, poking, making fun
Trying to assert and insert itself above hope and joy
Tearing and tossing nerves, frying them to medium rare

Pain is neither a figment of the imagination
Nor is it easily shifted or sifted away
"Give me your peace, your strength, your indie spirit,"
It demands, but your reserve shuts the door
Neither its banging, clanging nor sleep robbery is sufficient

You are holding your peace
Writing, soaring, singing in the nearly spent healthy percent
You go within and find a reservoir
A reservoir that spills golden gel on the grinding joints
Showers the seething neurons with nature's own hydrants

You sing lullabies among the dendrites, calming them
Cooing and extracting the balm from dopamine receptors
Cancelling orders for medically approved silencers
That knit nice rows of nothingness while *purling* knots in kidneys
You find the rivulets of perfection and calming waterfalls emerge. Amen

My living testimony to the benefits of, affirmative prayer, poetry therapy and Rev. Michael Beckwith's life visioning process in the midst of a back ailment in 2010. This was written throughout the night, November 24, 201, after I stopped taking the mind-boggling medications prescribed for me during the first week of November when breath-taking pain landed me in the hospital.

JOY COMES IN THE MORNING

Night is dark
> time of utter plight
> time to consider
> right and un-right

Night is vague
> about tomorrow's solutions
> about the day's retribution
> mighty against meek

Night is unending
> replaying daily pressures
> promoting comic gestures
> laughing at the lonely

Night is probing
> gentle places perturbing
> life forces disturbing
> challenging spiritual journey

Night is forever
> a prodder of tears and tenseness
> a splinter of hope and fierceness
> marching against the wild

Night is refreshing
> a time for reflecting
> opening doors and projecting

that joy comes in the morning

Joy comes in the morning
    to those walking in grace

Joy comes in the morning
    to those slowing their pace

Joy comes in the morning
    to those preparing to see God's face.

CHARLOTTE "SISTA C" FERRELL

Good Morning, God Morning

Good Morning, God Morning we lovingly check in
Through our daily Oath of Manifestation call, we inhale life in
We exhale and let go of things released from within
We share and declare the seven pillars and joyfully extend
Confirmation of the spiritual principles that exist without end

Gratitude, generosity, affluence, and compassion appear with grace
Ever setting new visions and helping others ascend to their place
Speaking our words, knowing with faith the promise will not erase
Professing, like Isaiah, that our word will not return void - we make haste
Seeking first the Kingdom we are opening doors within boundless space

Thank you, love you, goodbye, Ashe, and amen flow as an ending chorus
Forging new and ageless friendships like gold that is not porous
Closing the call where stories and prayers expressed the unexpected glorious

This prayer-poem was inspired by the Joy of Manifestation Family's morning "Oath" conference call now in its third year. The call was originated by Muriel Shabazz ALSP, and is based upon the "Oath of Manifestation" created and copyrighted by Rev. Dr. Cheryl Ward of Agape International University.

Chapter 10: Activities

"For your health as you bask in excellent health"

A. Quickly, list five true responses to the question, "How are you?"

1.

2.

3.

4.

5.

B. Explore the Health Team working in your body

1. First, take inventory. Mentally go through your body and do a *roll call*, identifying places that feel good and those that do not.

2. Visualize the areas that feel good and give thanks for them. Give them a tone; something you can hum, pat or otherwise sound. Make this sound as you think about the areas that do not feel as well. Picture and feel your whole body resonating or harmonizing with this tone.

3. Picture the area, cells or feelings that are ailing and imagine them as something treasured, like a bouquet of flowers, a trophy, lovely painting or something else you really enjoy. Send and speak love and appreciation instead of repeating sentiments such as *broken, aching, stupid, or ailing.*

4. Visualize yourself as the spokesperson to a conference of all the cells in your body. Thank them for their hard work and acknowledge times or ways you have ignored, strained or exhausted them. Ask them for your forgiveness and bless them with assurance you will attend to their needs more closely. Actually visualize the thousands of cells that serve you daily. Rally them to

greatness and shower them with appreciation. Initially, you may feel a little ridiculous doing this, but this practice, has significantly enabled me to trade pain killers for herbal remedies, occasional aspirin, or sometimes just a glass of water.

C. Re-imagine yourself

1. Take a deep look at yourself in a mirror and smile. Intentionally pull up any frown lines or wrinkles you see across your forehead. Greet yourself as a beautiful or handsome ambassador of joy, grateful for life and a body that has brought you this far. Smile at yourself frequently during the day and take time to notice from one day to the next that you are looking a little less tired, worried or in pain.

2. Use any of your devices with a camera and take a daily picture for two weeks. Usually when people say they don't like images of themselves it is because they are projecting/casting an unhappy look. Smile and watch your inner self smile back.

3. Picture yourself moving in perfect health as you adopt habits and eat foods that enable you to feel and look better. Whatever the ailment, it likely did not develop overnight. By seeing yourself as perfect, you allow healing balm to run across and seal pathways to old hurtful memories or self-concepts. You are more powerful than your past. The present of each new breath is that it carries oxygen to every cell; engage those refreshed cells in creative, beneficial pursuits.

D. Write-yourself 'right"

1. Journal or record statements about your journey toward wellness, wholeness or comfort with your body as a perfect emanation of God's love. Aim to express love, hope, kindness or joy in the midst of life's challenges. It is ok to express the times you feel frustrated, abandoned and disgruntled. Being able to identify these emotions, paint, acknowledge them and helps you to move on.

2. You guessed it. Try your hand at writing a 5-10-line poem about your journey.

Chapter 11
For you with love that is blessed from above

This is a great time to explore the wonders of love; to be in awe of its energy and healing power. What do you know about love? Most likely your sentiments or expectations go beyond syrupy commercials that suggest that love is best expressed through golden hearts and diamond rings. The love poems shared in *Heart Balm~Just for You* are among those I have written for people's engagement, wedding and anniversary celebrations. Some were also written via the faith principle of writing those things that are not as if they are.

Where does love come from. There are various religious and philosophical discussions around the issue of whether love need to be blessed by God, the state, or one's family. Some people reject their deepest feeling for someone because they do not achieve an external blessing. I believe that love is a treasured, miraculous feeling that comes from God and is limitless in its potential scope. We live in cultures and in the midst of media that nudge us to express it conditionally, measure it, selectively, withhold or award it. Exploring how we love ourselves, through meditation, journaling and poem-making is a vital step to finding and attracting the kind of loving relationships that feel like heaven on earth.

Happiness is Knowing

Happiness is a word so simple, it seems
It is the substance of many people's dreams
When happiness receives heavenly blessings
It leads to wedding rings.

Happiness is an experience we want friends to enjoy
It is sweeter than fruitcake,
More permanent than an expensive toy

Happiness comes from balancing life's ups and downs
It blossoms with daily smiles, not constant frowns
When happiness is bound to prayer
Love and laughter abounds

Happiness is knowing God gave you to me
Makes it truly easy
To make our pledge part of history

Messenger......Messenger

Messenger, messenger
Run and tell the news
Let go of all that is bound
Behold the good news

Messenger, messenger
Go forward with authority
Don't get distracted by the deceiver
There is no reason for your mission
to be anchored in sorrow

Messenger, messenger,
Send the word out from the street
Love is alive, you can feel it
as the palms sway in the breeze,
Turbulent death, get ready
to see your ultimate defeat.

The Messenger is moving
Old barriers are being rent
More energy and effort
On love is being spent
More empathy and sincerity
From our hearts is being sent

LOVE TIME~POEM TIME

Love time, poem time
Time for words from heaven to shine.
Love time, poem time
Time for words to pattern and rhyme
Time for words to wash the wounds
Bind the lashes and play bassoon

Love time, poem time
Time for poems, poets, singers
Time to untie all life's wringers.
Time for you to reveal to me
Unravel all your mystery.

Love time, poem time
Time for joy and utter grace
Rest from toiling in this place.
Place of poems, place of words
Place for love instead of swords.
Love time, poem time.
Poem time, love time.

Included on the Just for You Cd, this is a popular performance poem where folk dance or 'chime in' with the fantastic tempo-shifting tune Greg Moon and Gabriel Bibbs created to flow with my poem..

DOUBLE YES

They keep asking 'are we sure'?
Did we take enough time to make up our minds?
Did we get enough education?
Or, have enough fun?
The answer is *"Yes,* double *Yes."*

They ask if we have the sustainability
To last until perpetuity
Will we scramble and fuss,
Or can we hold on to "us"
When the tests of time begin to unfold
The answer is "Yes, double Yes."

What of the ties we have to careers and our crowd...
Shopping dates, movie nights, bowling leagues, card parties,
And better yet, customary family occasions
Can we re-schedule, budget and adjust our priorities?
The answer is "Yes, double Yes."

Do we take each other, with our fragile feelings
To have and to hold – to treasure like gold,
Until we slip into to life's higher ceiling?
The answer is "Yes, double Yes."

THANK GOD FOR YOU IN MY LIFE

FROM this "Yo baby, hey woman
Hip-hop, flip-flop,
Steady half-stepping"- world...
YOU came into my life.

FROM this "Hey daddy,
Gimmie this, prove that,
How much you got, kind of world ...
YOU came into my life.

When you came into my life the strife receded.
When you came into my life the joy interceded.

When you came into my life, I lost my chief gripe
When you came into my life, my destiny was suddenly ripe

With you in my life- everyday has light
With you in my life -my future is bright

With you in my life, both night and day are all right
With you in my life, even quarrels are a delight

With you in my life, God's mission is so clear
His words remove the fear because, you both are holding me dear.

With you in my life, God's promise is manifest
His words confirm the rest because you are a gift of his best

CHARLOTTE "SISTA C" FERRELL

This poem is dedicated to those who find the love and consecrate it in marital bliss. It was first written and presented at a wedding, with my son, Ato alternating the lines with me, then recorded with arranger-musician, Hilliard Wilson. It is included on the Just for You Cd.

SENT TO YOU WITH LOVE

Today many people will open their mouths and say:
"Happy Valentine's Day", "Happy Anniversary",
"Happy _____ Day"
"I love you – will you be mine?"

But today, I pray
That the women of the world
the men of the world
the children of the world
Will open our hearts

Open our hearts' shutters
and let our 'little lights' shine
Open our hearts' trap doors
and eject hurt or anger
Open our hearts' windows
and let hope beams radiate

Today we will take down our heart barricades
and let happiness overflow
Open our hearts' mirrors
and beam ourselves some love
Open our hearts' valves
and let Love restore the lining.
Hydrate our pores with essential
Jasmine and myrrh scented oil

Today this poem has come to me
as a gift, out of the blue
So, as treasured as frankincense,
I am sending it on to you

HOW BEAUTIFUL IT IS

How beautiful it is when two hearts can intertwine
Hold on to each other's beats at midnight
When two souls can spend evenings clasping hands
      Clasping pieces of the past
      Clasping and cherishing treasured pieces of creative characters
      Clasping hope and warmth in the chill of a Parisian night

How beautiful it is when two spirits can sing
Sing songs that can be heard by fellow travelers flocked and un-flocked
Open doors, say, "Won't you come in...we have a few treats for you."
Close pages to an era with a gift of verse
A fond goodbye shared without shame

How beautiful it is when one or two can be gathered on one accord
Shelter others' dreams with pictures, pen and virtual tools
Build new frameworks for old words
Make word pictures that pat, nurture, bind, and blend
Cause to find a wonderful platform
For the collective dreamers to spring forth

How beautiful it is when one has a heart to share
Your heart from autumn, to winter, through the spring
To a summer of warm harvests and languishing love
How beautiful it is that Andrea met George and
George met Andrea and they cared up a storm
May your storm seed endless love to estranged hearts everywhere

When my man kisses me

Champagne.
Chocolate Cake
Chicken A La King
Strawberry Shortcake
Shrimp and Lobster Bisque
But don't lick your lips yet
I'd trade them all in
       for a kiss from my man.

When my man kisses me
A shiver goes straight to my knees
The sun trades places with the moon
And the stars want to shine at noon

When my man kisses me
Chile, my heart sings for glee
Flowers start blooming all over town
And even the meanest folks lose their frowns

When my man kisses me
My heart bounds up a tree
The chef finds what's been missing
To earn his dish a royal blessing

When my man kisses me
It's beyond what you ordinarily see
Colors of the rainbow pass my eyes
And, in the kitchen, something fries

Apple crisps. Custard. Cinnamon Cake
Chocolate hearts are all that bake
When my man kisses me!

CHARLOTTE "SISTA C" FERRELL

Chapter 11: Activities
For you with love that is blessed from above

Cards, programs and songs throughout our culture re-iterate the words, "love blessed from above. Yet, we rarely discuss what that really means.

1. Brainstorm with a notepad, and write out what "love blessed from above means" to you.
2. Are your thoughts cynical, humorous or sentimental?
3. At this point you have exercised your writing muscles somewhat. Put a pen to paper or fingers to keys and write a three paragraph essay on whether you think love is or needs to be blessed, and where you think the blessing comes from.

This third activity generates much conversation in a small group. If you have a partner or small group with whom you feel comfortable discussing this topic, trade essays and discuss these questions.

4. Observe some older people in your family or community who have been together a long time. Ask them if they would feel comfortable having you write a poem about their love or relationship. I have personally found this to bring a couple so much fun- reminiscing and giving pointers on what they think would be good or memorable things to say. It also gives you a sweet source of heart balm and hope for having a relationship like this unfold in your life.

Chapter 12
For You With Bliss That Never Goes Amiss

Say,' bliss', aloud within a small group you're likely to experience a rippling pool of varying sentiments ebbing into being. Bliss carried through the media mill translates into fleeting moments of sensuous pleasure or mindless rapture. From the spiritual realm, Rev. Michael Bernard Beckwith describes it as *a zone of comfort and contentment with the joy of being love, not' in love', but love itself.*

Over time, I have stopped pursuing the "airy" feeling of storybook bliss that sweeps me off my feet and sends butterflies fluttering around my heart. Bliss is the sweetness of a day spent laughing with my grandsons, or playing a table game with my adult kids. It is riding in the car and not getting lost or side swiped by a distracted driver. It's hearing a singer run the scales and soar from octave to octave. Bliss is watching musicians sway with joy as they bring music from another realm. At the end of the day it is feeling good about interactions with others, not having to worry about whether I was just, honest or truthful.

I am pleased to share sentiments on the simple joy of bliss without a fast talking list of negative side effects. This final chapter shares blissful sentiments that soar from the serious to the sensuous, the zany to the profoundly peaceful. This culminating chapter confers a blessing of bliss - *just for you*.

FOR ALL TO ENJOY

Bliss Is gone amiss
It is promised on paper labels
Bumped and broadcast
From WiFi to HD to you and me

Bliss sounds so tasty
So engaging, bouncy and beautiful
No matter the price tag
We must have bliss

But you have the power to
Impart blessings amidst your bliss
To share feelings wholly sincere
To share songs that makes love clear

You are the bliss painter,
An architect of joy
Building foundations and fountains
With stability and serenity for all to enjoy

CHARLOTTE "SISTA C" FERRELL

You Are, I Am, We Are

You are my toast, I am your butter
You are my lettuce, I am your tomatoes

You are my vehicle, I am your safety belt
You are my Popeye, I am your spinach

You are my cup of tea, I am your honey
You are my picnic basket, I am your sandwiches and soda

You are my ocean, I am your yacht
You are my jetliner, I am your rockets

You are my sand, I am your sandcastle
You are my headlights, I am your brakes

You are my sun, I am your star
You are my chair, I am your cushions

You are my strawberry short cake; I am your whipped cream
You are my root beer; I am the ice cream for your float

You are my music, I am your lyrics
You are an answer to my prayers, I am yours.

Colorless Intentions

Colorless intentions on a life-size palette
Holding rich hues of brown, emerald,
                   aquamarine, golden russet, crimson
Faceless across virtual space
Yet communicating smiling eyes
Intense hands. Driven Spirit
Patiently listening to an aspiring client's wish list
                Mindful of time. Counting down minutes
                Keenly aware of the pending deadline

You nudge promising pieces together
Goal 1... Goal 2, go for it
Never mind the short yardage
Creative pursuits have their own time tables
Spirit time. All in due time
Results triumphantly flow
Milestones march across the screen,
                from bitmaps to jpegs
Story boards to Out- looking the real thing

Blessings, Harmony, Prosperity, Joy
You work magic with keystrokes, like a toy
Intricately your colorless intentions
Have crafted a palette of precious dimensions

Where Is It?

Sometimes in the course of human events
We have occasion to ask, "Where is it?"
Where is my soul, what has become of it?
I thought it was here, but someone said it was there.
I can't seem to tell if it is anywhere.

If Dr. Seuss were summoned, he might ask,
Did you leave it in a car? Did you put it in a jar?
Did you see it in the rain? Did you feel it through your pain?
Do you think it is in the air? Do you really, truly care?

Over time this is what I have come to see
My soul is nestled comfortably within me
It greeted me at birth
It will accompany me from this earth
It is the gift I can never return
Keeping it in integrity is the bliss of life's sojourn.

STICKING AND HOLDING

Stick and move
Stick and move
"Stick and move," the boxing trainers say

Believe and hold
Believe and hold
"Believe and hold," the spiritual teachers say

Sticking and believing
Holding onto faith
Be-ing you as you encounter
Life's blissful transformation

Honoring the trainer and the teacher
Consciousness fully comforted
Ego harnessed to let endless possibilities run
You flow and glow, sticking and believing

I Am Going to Love this Day Happy

I am going to love this day happy, all the day long
I am going to love this day happy, the whole day long
The sun has not yet blossomed today
It set hours and hours ago
But, I am going to love this day happy all the day long

Happiness and health rise from slumber together
Happiness swirls though hope-kissed wind
Wafts far and near with energy to spend
Cools simmering concrete sidewalks
While whistling songs to birds in flight
Happiness, through the rhythm of living hearts,
Soothes and calms newborns
Salutes those returning home

I am going to love this day happy, all the day long
Because it is a priceless gift, a note from Mother Love
A stay of execution from an ancient Judge
This day is yet in germination
It is in the final stages of gestation
I am so honored, so tenderly grateful
To be a midwife, a soul trusted to catch it, as it crests
To catch it as it parts the clouds and bursts forth into waiting hands

This newborn I will greet with clean hands and an open heart
This newborn I will nurture, caress and claim as my own
This emerging, welcomed day has no siblings, no competitors

This emerging day is lovingly birthed in searing heat,
It is pregnant with promises that I will nurse
Nurse, and nurture for the eyes and hearts I touch today.
I am going to love this day happy, all the day long.

Integrals of Life

Listen. Even the birds notice
They are chirp-warping the message across the medians
They feel it, are buoyed higher by it
It is such an integral part of life

Words, pledges, promises and deeds
As seasons and circumstances change can you keep your creed?
Away from the spotlights
Running beneath the radar
The bliss of your integrity rides the high waves

Water rippling over stones, through sand
Tracing patterns locked into the land
Confidence and courage walking hand in hand
Resolved to sustain bliss through chance and change

Inching its way like tulip bulbs
Assurance in vows, affirmations and confirmations
Lips breaking through peat moss and southern loam
Sending elegant little goblets above the ground

Integrals of life
Intense, infinite beings
Brining joy, sustaining hope
Cascading new conviction for commitment without sorrow

(This poem is inspired by the answer Rev. Michael Beckwith gave when I asked his definition of bliss. He said, "It is being in integrity with your soul.")

Re-birthing I Worthiness

You are the beloved of your innermost heart
With each beat a thunderous reminder sounds
Yet sometimes it falls into the abyss
The abyss of misconceptions about "I" worthiness
The abyss of mistrust fed by ill conceptions
Of how marvelous it would be if you felt fantastic about "I"

You are the "I" that has smelled the sacred essence of fertile dreams
You are the "I" that has felt brilliance brimming over with solutions
Solutions to family matters, financial matters, environmental matters
Solutions to the issues of the day that matter most for human survival
You are the "I" that has voluntarily surrendered its voice,
Surrendered its power,
Surrendered its sweetness

Now step into the bliss of birthing "I" from its cocoon
Now step into the bliss of birthing the fruit of your Yes
Now step into the bliss of acknowledging "I" love with content
Acknowledging love and appreciation for your gifts as "I"
Acknowledging love and appreciation for the "I" in your integrity
Acknowledging love and appreciation for the "I" that has:
Abundant creativity, abundant health, abundant joy,
Abundant generosity, abundant prosperity, and abundant peace
And so it is for "I" and "I".

CHARLOTTE "SISTA C" FERRELL

Chapter 12: Activities
"For You With Bliss That Never Goes Amiss"

How blissful do you feel? The activities here are introspective and playful. Try them and reflect upon how they make you feel.

1. Think about how you feel about the word bliss. Write a sentence about it. _____

   _____

2. How do you feel about your "word?" Do you hold off agreeing to do things unless they feel 'right' with you. Consider keeping a "word log" for a few days and observe whether you feel blissful or regretful over things you have agreed to do.

3. Try your hand at writing three different poems about bliss or feeling blissful. Write one that is playful; one that is sensuous; and one that expresses unconditional love.

4. If you would like to explore how your concept of 'bliss' aligns or contrasts with that of someone close to you, share and discuss the above three activities.

Commentary

Perhaps you've read and done activities from all 12 chapters of this book. Perhaps not. Regardless of the number you may have done, I would love to hear from you and know whether they were a "balm", "the bomb" or simply beneficial to your life. Feel free to contact me at **charlotte@csistacf.com**

About the Author

Charlotte "Sista C" Ferrell draws upon 20 years of international experience as a Health Educator, Registered Dietitian and writer to create engaging courses, retreats, events and movies. She passionately uses her creative arts skills to promote healthy lifestyles, support people in recovery and encourage optimum health inter-generationally. Along with providing traditional medical diet therapy, she introduces people to such complimentary health concepts as mindfulness, guided visioning, and health writing. During her 14 years as a consultant for US VETS in Inglewood, CA, she has used food demonstrations, classes, poetry writing and and events to promote healthy behaviors. As a national Food Safety Manager course administrator, she uses improv, "reader's theater" and videos to help people with low literacy levels understand complex concepts and pass certification exams. She collaborates with community and faith organizations to host poetry writing and peace art events for children and adults, especially during the 'Season of Non-Violence' and International Peace Days. She has been invited to do poetry performances and conduct workshops at correctional and convalescent facilities, worksites and festivals. Charlotte is an award-winning instructor, poet and filmmaker:

- 2016 Honors Graduate, Digital Cinema and Video Production, Art Institute of CA-Hollywood
- July, 2016, Los Angeles CineFest, Semi-Finalist, narrative short film, "Sisters out of the Box".
- 2015 Faculty of the Year (Humanities and Science) University of Phoenix, So Cal Campuses
- "Revive & Reverb" Poetry Tribute written and presented at the opening of the Harlem Renaissance West Artists installation at the African America Museum, Macy's, Los Angeles
- 2014 International Festival of Film and Cinematic Arts (IFFCA), Laurel for, "One Score and 17 Nights".
- 2012 "Ambassadors of Peace and Love", Children's Spoken Word, Poetry month event, CPUMC

Charlotte "Sista C" Ferrell's work has been recognized by Who's Who of Entrepreneurs (2001-2), Who's Who of Distinguished Alumni (2015-16), and published in the Poetry Hall of Fame, Sparrowgrass Publishing, SoulVisions Anthology: "Deep River Rhythms", The Kansas City Star, the Toronto Globe and Mail, L.A. City News, and the National Library of Poetry. During 2015 she was given a "Faculty of the Year" award by the College of Humanities and Science at University of Phoenix (SoCal), and in 2016, she was presented with Certificates of Recognition as a creative artist from the Mayor of Los Angeles, and the Mayor of Redondo Beach.